D1029335

The Pleasures of Reading in an Age of Distraction

THE

PLEASURES

of

READING

in an

AGE

of

DISTRACTION

Alan Jacobs

OXFORD
UNIVERSITY PRESS

OXFORD
UNIVERSITY PRESS

Oxford University Press, Inc., publishes works that further
Oxford University's objective of excellence
in research, scholarship, and education.

Oxford   New York
Auckland   Cape Town   Dar es Salaam   Hong Kong   Karachi
Kuala Lumpur   Madrid   Melbourne   Mexico City   Nairobi
New Delhi   Shanghai   Taipei   Toronto

With offices in
Argentina   Austria   Brazil   Chile   Czech Republic   France   Greece
Guatemala   Hungary   Italy   Japan   Poland   Portugal   Singapore
South Korea   Switzerland   Thailand   Turkey   Ukraine   Vietnam

Copyright © 2011 by Alan Jacobs

Published by Oxford University Press, Inc.
198 Madison Avenue, New York, New York 10016

www.oup.com

Oxford is a registered trademark of Oxford University Press

Jacobs, Alan, 1958
The pleasures of reading in an age of distraction / Alan Jacobs.
p. cm.
Includes bibliographical references.
ISBN 978-0-19-974749-8
1. Reading.   2. Self-culture.   3. Study skills.   I. Title.
PN83.J36 2011
028'.8–dc22   2010034350

1 3 5 7 9 8 6 4 2
Printed in the United States of America
on acid-free paper

For my students, with whom I have read, and will read, so much

Caveat lector ☞ Those who have always disliked reading, or who have been left indifferent by it, may find little of interest here. But those who have caught a glimpse of what reading can give—pleasure, wisdom, joy— even if that glimpse came long ago, are the audience for whom this book was written.

The Pleasures of Reading in an Age of Distraction

Yes, we can! ☞ A while back my teenage son drifted into the room where I was reading, tilting his head to catch the title of the book in my hands. It was that venerable classic *How to Read a Book*, by Mortimer Adler and Charles van Doren. "Oh man," he said, "I had to read that in school last year. Maybe I learned something about how to read a book, but after that I never *wanted* to read a book again."

In 1940 Mortimer Adler published the first edition of *How to Read a Book* and was, he later commented, surprised at its immediate and lasting popularity. Although Adler was unabashedly elitist in some respects—the belief that some books are Great Books and that those are the books most worth reading animated his whole life—*How to Read a Book* belongs to a fine tradition of American populism. The conviction underlying the whole enterprise was that you need not have an expensive university education in order to be a skillful reader of even the most challenging texts. Rather, you just need a bit of guidance—a single volume's worth of recommended strategies and tactics—and you can take it from there, following your own path to erudition, making yourself worthy of the Great Tradition of which Adler himself was but a humble acolyte. Adler's guide was to reading what Charles Atlas's "Dynamic Tension" program was to bodybuilding: a common-sense, practical program for the average American with some do-it-yourself gumption. (There are passages of exhortation in *How to Read a Book* that sound quite a lot like Charles Atlas: "With nothing but the power of your own mind, you operate on the symbols before you in such a way that you gradually lift yourself from a state of understanding less to one of understanding more." This is the intellectual equivalent of Atlas's "dynamic tension" approach to bodybuilding, which rather than using weights "pits muscle against muscle.") And in an age when relatively few Americans attended college, and still fewer attended colleges with a liberal-arts emphasis, there was, it turned out, a great hunger for the kind of confident instruction Adler offered.

When, three decades later, Adler enlisted Charles Van Doren to help him revise his guide to reading, the American social fabric had altered considerably. Thanks in large part to the postwar GI Bill, which paid college tuition for returning soldiers, a much higher percentage of Americans were attending college. One might think that in such circumstances Adler's direction would be less valuable. But, he argued, universities focused so much on the dissemination of facts and so little on the pursuit of understanding that the reading abilities of the American public had not been much improved by the rise in college attendance. Moreover, something else had occurred since 1940: television. Americans were becoming ever more distracted and ever less instructed; reading was becoming an increasingly unfamiliar and indeed unnatural practice; and therefore his book remained as timely as it had ever been.

In this claim Adler was probably right. But what would he have said if in 1972 he had been granted a vision of the next thirty years of American history? Seeing the innumerably greater distractions available to us, he may well have given up the cause of reading as a lost one. After all, in 1972 few Americans had access to more than four television stations, and the only computers were elephantine hulks locked in the basements of universities and a few large corporations.

But despite the lamentations of many contemporary Jeremiahs, the cause of reading is not a lost one by any means. There are millions of devoted readers in America, as can be evidenced by the hundreds of enormous Borders and Barnes & Noble bookstores (despite the recent struggles of those chains), by the huge success of Amazon.com as a seller of books, by Oprah's Book Club, and by the most recent NEA survey of reading in America, which reveals a surprising uptick in the reading of literary fiction and other long-form works.[*]

And consider this: in January 2008 Steve Jobs, the head of Apple Computer, was interviewed by reporters from the *New York Times*, and while Jobs was primarily interested in celebrating Apple's newest products, he was willing to announce his views on other matters as well. For instance, Amazon.com's then-new electronic reading device, the Kindle: "It doesn't matter how good or bad the product is, the fact is that people don't read anymore," he said. "Forty percent of the people in the U.S. read one book or less

---

[*] *"Reading on the Rise*, the National Endowment for the Arts' new report, documents a significant turning point in recent American cultural history. For the first time in over a quarter-century, our survey shows that literary reading has risen among adult Americans. After decades of declining trends, there has been a decisive and unambiguous increase among virtually every group measured in this comprehensive national survey" (http://www.nea.gov/research/ReadingonRise.pdf). The surveys on which the report was based were conducted in 2008.

last year. The whole conception is flawed at the top because people don't read anymore." Two years later he introduced Apple's new product, the iPad, and emphasized the gadget's ties to Apple's new online bookstore and its excellence as a medium for reading newspaper, magazines, and yes, even books. I don't think a highly exploitable clientele of readers spontaneously self-generated between 2008 and 2010.

I meet and talk to and hear from many readers: I regularly get emails and letters from readers of my previous books, and those readers seem to cover a remarkably broad spectrum of education and experience. Just in the past few weeks I have heard from three readers of my biography of C. S. Lewis: an email from a Canadian college student who had written a long post about it on her blog, a letter from a high school student in Florida who had typed and sent to me a one-page review of the book (she liked it overall, but found some passages confusing), and a long handwritten letter from an elderly woman in New York who half-a-century ago had corresponded with Lewis and wanted to give me an account of it. These are limited sorts of conversations, of course, but when I get to talk more fully with readers I discover that for all their enthusiasm they often lack confidence: they wonder whether they are reading well, with focus and attentiveness, with discretion and discernment.

This uncertainty spans the generations but comes in different flavors. I find myself particularly intrigued by younger people who have heard their cohort called "The Dumbest Generation," who are continually told that their addiction to multiple simultaneous stimuli renders them incapable of the seriously focused and single-minded attention that the reading of big thick books requires. Some of them are defiant in response to such charges, but most at least half-believe them. Told over and over again that they can't read, they begin to wonder why they should even try. It's not just teenagers and twenty-somethings who sound such a note; I have heard talk like this from people up to forty and in a few cases older. Many of them say that they used to be able to read but since becoming habituated to online reading and the short bursts of attention it encourages—or demands—simply can't sit down with a book anymore. They fidget; they check their iPhones for email and Twitter updates. Thus Nicholas Carr:

> Over the past few years I've had an uncomfortable sense that some-one, or something, has been tinkering with my brain, remapping the neural circuitry, reprogramming the memory. My mind isn't going—so far as I can tell—but it's changing. I'm not thinking the way I used to think. I can feel it most strongly when I'm reading. Immersing myself in a book or a lengthy article used to be easy. My mind would get caught up in the narrative or the turns of the argu-ment, and I'd spend hours strolling through long stretches of prose. That's rarely the case anymore. Now my concentration often starts to drift after two or three pages. I get fidgety, lose the thread, begin looking for something else to do. I feel as if I'm always dragging my wayward brain back to the text. The deep reading that used to come naturally has become a struggle.

And he concludes, mournfully, "I miss my old brain." (I'll have more to say about Carr's particular predicament later in this book.)

All of these people *can* read, of course. Those who never have done so can learn, and those who have lost the habit can reacquire it.* The plasticity of the brain is an amazing thing, but training it

---

*It is noteworthy that, in spite of the worries I have mentioned, most people not only think well of the act of reading but, a team of sociologists from Northwestern University report, fully expect to be doing more of it in the future: "More than nine out of ten are convinced that reading is 'a good use of your time'.... And they think

requires effort and patience. I am aware that my "you can do it" rhetoric here echoes Adler and Charles Atlas, not to mention Barack Obama and Bob the Builder. But the American DIY tradition is by no means a contemptible one; it just needs, especially when applied to reading, a little updating. The Adler–Van Doren model, with its decision-tree model of engagement—"If book is of Type 1, apply reading technique C"—and its strongly legislative tone is not ideally suited to today's habits of mind.

Adler and Van Doren are strict taskmasters. A word that appears often in their account is "obligation," and its business end is generally pointed at the book's reader. Their book is a "practical" one, they remind us, intended to foster certain specific results, and "the reader of a practical book has a special obligation with respect to it." If "the reader of a practical book accepts the ends it proposes and agrees that the means recommended are appropriate and effective," then he or she is obliged to follow the book's instructions. It's hard not to have some anxiety about what Adler and Van Doren might do to us if we fail in that obligation.

There's an odd passage in *How to Read a Book* when Adler and Van Doren are discussing the reading of "canonical" texts. By this, they mean not just religious texts, sacred books, but any books that

---

they ought to be able to read more, for very few people find reading 'too hard to do'....They expect to read more in the future. When asked, 'Do you think you'll find yourself reading more in the months and years ahead, reading less, or is the amount of reading you do probably going to stay the same,' 45% said more, 3% less, and 51% the same....People particularly intend to read more materials that are educational or will improve their lives, such as nonfiction books, newspapers, and the Bible. A British survey finds that people actually believe they are reading more. 'Despite competition from new media, and increasing pressure on people's leisure time, relatively few people think they are reading books less now than five years ago. Most (80%) claim to be reading about the same or more.'"

carry absolute authority within a given community. In discussing this kind of reading Adler and Van Doren retrieve the notion of readerly obligation and give it some extra punch:

> The faithful reader of a canonical book is obliged to make sense out of it and to find it true in one or another sense of "true." If he cannot do this by himself, he is obliged to go to someone who can. This may be a priest or rabbi, or it may be his superior in the party hierarchy, or it may be his professor. In any case, he is obliged to accept the resolution of his problem that is offered him. He reads essentially without freedom; but in return for this he gains a kind of satisfaction that is possibly never obtained when reading other books.

When I read the first part of this passage, I discerned a certain skepticism toward the claims made for canonical texts; but that last sentence—"a kind of satisfaction that is possibly never obtained when reading other books"—sounds rather wistful to me, as though Adler and Van Doren wouldn't altogether mind exerting that kind of authority themselves. And that impression is strengthened by the passage I've already quoted in which they stress the obligations of readers to the very kind of book they have written.

I wouldn't be surprised if many readers of *How to Read a Book* actually like this tone: it is the strongly worded lecture that helps stiffen the backbone, strengthen the resolve. (George Orwell tells the story of a childhood schoolmate of his who did poorly on an examination and afterward wished, mournfully, that he had been caned before it so that he would have studied harder.) After all, among those who wish they were better readers, a good number do tend to think of reading as a means of self-improvement: it is thanks to them that *How to Read a Book* is still in print. One can certainly read in order to build up intellectual muscles, and I will have a bit to say about that in the pages that follow. But I will have a lot more to say about other matters. Forget for a moment *how* books should be read: *Why* should they be read? The first reason—the first sequentially in the story that follows but also the first in order of importance—is that reading books can be intensely pleasurable. Reading is one of the great human delights. And the Charles Atlases of reading rarely remember this.

Mortimer Adler's coauthor, Charles Van Doren, may have realized that there was something unfortunately dutiful about *How to Read a Book*, because in 1985 he published *The Joy of Reading: A Passionate Guide to 189 of the World's Best Authors and Their Works*. Adler himself commended the book in a blurb, as did the legendary editor Clifton Fadiman: "Mr. Van Doren is that rarity, a truly well read man who reads not for professional purposes but for pleasure. His book spurs us on to explore more deeply and joyfully the infinitely varied terrain of good books." But for all the talk here of joy, passion, and pleasure, the spell of readerly responsibility is a difficult one to dismiss, as can be seen in Fadiman's own book, *The New Lifetime Reading Plan: The Classical Guide to World Literature*, the key word here being *Plan*.* Indeed, Van Doren's guide, however passionate it may be, sticks with the canonical authors almost as methodically as Fadiman's does, and concludes the book with, yes, a "Ten-Year Reading Plan," whose contents and sequence are "more than merely suggestive." Now, Van Doren may earn some populist *bona fides* by adding to his list, in a revised 2008 edition, J. K. Rowling and, of all people, Carl Hiaasen—but there's something odd about such writers ending up on a *list*, which is intrinsically directive, instructive, authoritative.

---

*Fadiman published the first version of this book, called *Clifton Fadiman's Lifetime Reading Plan*, in 1960.

This self-help, self-improvement model of reading seems deeply embedded in American cultural life: even Michael Dirda, a wonderfully sensitive and humane reader-critic, in his *Book by Book*, can't resist offering a master list of sixteen works and asserting that if you just read these particular texts with care, "nearly all of world literature will be an open book to you." Really? "Nearly all of world literature," and I just have to read these sixteen? Cause yields effect so automatically?

(It's the kind of thing Americans love to believe, and have for a long time: in 1835 the Christian evangelist Charles Finney, later the first president of Oberlin College, affirmed that "the connection between the right use of means for a [religious] revival and a revival is as philosophically [i.e., scientifically] sure as between the right use of means to raise grain and a crop of wheat. I believe, in fact, it is more certain, and there are fewer instances of failure." Growing wheat, converting people to Christianity, opening the whole world of literature to people—it's all just a matter of appropriate instrumentation, of applying the proper technique, of carefully following the instructions.)

It would be easy enough to dismiss Adler and Van Doren and Fadiman et al. for pedantry, but as I have already indicated the American reading public, or a significant chunk of it anyway, can't take its readerly pleasure straight but has to cut it with a sizable splash of duty. Books that aren't certifiably good for you are, in this way of thinking, to be suspected—and to read for "entertainment," or the sheer pleasure of the thing, verges on the morally unjustifiable. Thomas C. Foster's *How to Read Literature Like a Professor* and *How to Read Novels Like a Professor* tap into many of the same anxieties: they suggest that reading is best done by highly trained, professionally accredited experts; the implicit promise is that such expertise is at least partially transferable to the ordinary reader.

As a professor of literature, I must say that when I first saw Foster's books I thought, "Read like a professor? Good Lord, anything but that!" (Although, of course, Foster's imagined professor is an ideal one.) I sympathize with the view of academic reading that the novelist Zadie Smith articulated in an interview a few years ago:

> My main feeling is that my time as a student, especially my last year, was genuinely the happiest period of my life. But—BIG BUT—there were many things about academic life that I found unbearably oppressive and absurd. There's so much of one's real lived experiences that you have to leave at the gates. There's something about English departments in particular—a kind of desperate need to be serious, to be professional, to police this very ambiguous and necessarily amorphous act, reading—that I find hard to deal with. . . . I always feel a disappointment coming out of English departments, as if all these brilliant people are gathered and poised to study something and all they have to study is . . . *these things? Novels? But they're so . . . smooshy.* . . . It depresses me, how embarrassed some people seem to be about novels, how much they want them to be something else.

But however attractive this promise of expertise—or the similarly directive step-by-step approach of Adler and Van Doren, or the eat-your-vegetables lists of approved authoritative texts provided by Fadiman—can be for some, for others it only makes reading feel like drudgery. My son is one such person: it was the aroma of Responsibility, Obligation, and Virtue emanating from *How to Read a Book* that sent him fleeing. And there are many people like my son among the ranks of diffident readers, embarrassed non-readers, and guilt-stricken ex-readers—especially among natives or long habitués of the digital world. So I want to offer a very different model of what reading can be all about.

Whim ☞ Several times a year I get requests from people—usually students, but also friends and acquaintances, and even total strangers who have managed to find my email address—who want reading lists. "Dear Professor Jacobs, could you please give me your recommendations for what I should read this summer?" Or, "Dear Professor, in your opinion what are the ten most important books that every educated person should read?" I dislike that second question for reasons that are probably already clear, but the first I can't bring myself to dislike at all, since it's really a compliment in the form of a question.

Nonetheless, I never comply with these requests.

There are a few reasons why, and both of them are related to my views about the value and pleasure of reading. First, if people just want a list of the Greatest Hits of Western Literature (the *Iliad*, the *Divine Comedy*, *Hamlet*, *Paradise Lost*, *The Brothers Karamazov*), they can get that anywhere. Indeed, they probably already know what items go on that list. So presumably they want something else, though it's not always clear to me, and perhaps not to them, precisely what. My sense is that they want either books that have been particularly important to *me*—that's where the compliment comes in—or else the kind of book that gets written up in magazines as a "forgotten masterpiece." But there are many, many books that would fit into that latter category; and there is little reason to think that a book will be especially interesting or helpful to someone else just because *I* like it. Another person may not have my inclinations, interests, or personal needs.

Now, if people came to me and said, "Here's a list of ten of my favorite books—can you think of some others I'm likely to enjoy?" I would be more likely—and better prepared—to answer. But that rarely happens, which is unfortunate: as much as I dislike the general, abstract, decontextualized lists that people tend to ask for, I love making recommendations to people I know and

whose interests and tastes are familiar to me. Not long ago, as
I was romping through Neal Stephenson's vast science-fiction opus
Anathem, I kept thinking of a friend whose major passions are woven
into that book. So as soon as I finished the story I ran right out to
my local Borders, bought a second copy, and delivered it to his door
with an exhortation to read it as soon as was humanly possible.
I wasn't sure, of course, whether my friend would in the end like the
book, but I knew he would be fascinated by much that happens in it,
and, above all, I knew that we would have some enjoyable conversations about Stephenson's story. Thus Rudyard Kipling: "One can't
prescribe books, even the best books, to people unless one knows a
good deal about each individual person. If a man is keen on reading,
I think he ought to open his mind to some older man who knows
him and his life, and to take his advice in the matter, and above all, to
discuss with him the first books that interest him."

In such a context of friendship and mutual interest, the making of recommendations is a pleasure. Outside of that, it quickly
becomes an onerous (and perhaps pointless) duty, and I don't like
mixing reading with onerous duties. Moreover, in many cases
these requests have little to do with actually reading anything, but
rather with *having read*—with the desire to say, "Yes, now I can
check that one off." In his marvelous memoir *Hunger of Memory*,
Richard Rodriguez describes how he once experienced this curious compulsion: "In the fourth grade," he writes, "I embarked on
a grandiose reading program." He asked his teachers for lists of
"important books," which he then began dutifully to read, without
having any sense of what made the books worthwhile.

> I decided to record in a notebook the themes of the books that
> I read. After reading *Robinson Crusoe*, I wrote that its theme was "the
> value of learning to live by oneself." When I completed *Wuthering
> Heights*, I noted the danger of "letting emotions get out of control."

Reading these brief moralistic appraisals usually left me disheart-
ened. I couldn't believe that they were really the source of reading's
value. But for many more years, they constituted the only means
I had of describing to myself the educational value of books.

It is true, of course, that adult readers are unlikely to be quite
as naïve as the young Rodriguez was: the people who ask me
for reading recommendations aren't likely to write the themes
of books in a notebook or on three-by-five cards. But the difference is not as great as one might suppose; the sense of obligation
is much the same. Rodriguez's experience of reading, say, Plato's
Republic might not be altogether alien to that of many of his elders:
"I needed to keep looking at the book jacket comments to remind
myself what the text was about. Nevertheless, . . . I looked at
every word of the text. And by the time I reached the last word,
I convinced myself that I had read *The Republic*. In a ceremony of
great pride, I solemnly crossed Plato off my list."

So one reason I usually decline to give reading recommendations
is that I don't want to encourage such habits of mind. But there's
a positive counterpart to this negative reason: my commitment to
one dominant, overarching, nearly definitive principle for reading:
Read at Whim. I learned this principle from the essayist and poet
Randall Jarrell, who once met a scholar, a learned man and a critic,
who commented that he read Rudyard Kipling's novel *Kim* every
year. Jarrell's response:

The critic said that once a year he read *Kim*; and he read *Kim*, it was
plain, at whim: not to teach, not to criticize, just for love—he read
it, as Kipling wrote it, just because he liked to, wanted to, couldn't
help himself. To him it wasn't a means to a lecture or article, it was
an end; he read it not for anything he could get out of it, but for
itself. And isn't this what the work of art demands of us? The work

of art, Rilke said, says to us always: You must change your life. It demands of us that we too see things as ends, not as means—that we too know them and love them for their own sake. This change is beyond us, perhaps, during the active, greedy, and powerful hours of our lives; but during the contemplative and sympathetic hours of our reading, our listening, our looking, it is surely within our power, if we choose to make it so, if we choose to let one part of our nature follow its natural desires. So I say to you, for a closing sentence, *Read at whim! read at whim!*

Now, it might seem at first that Jarrell contradicts himself in this passage: first he commends reading a book "for itself," then he commends reading a book because it tells me that I must change my life. But the contradiction is only apparent. The book that simply demands to be read, for no good reason, is asking us to change our lives by putting aside what we usually think of as good reasons. It's asking us to stop calculating. It's asking us to do something for the plain old delight and interest of it, not because we can justify its place on the mental spreadsheet or accounting ledger (like the one Benjamin Franklin kept) by which we tote up the value of our actions.

Early in *How to Read a Book*, Adler and Van Doren explain that reading is something one does primarily for *information* and *understanding*. But they then add, somewhat apologetically,

Of course, there is still another goal of reading, besides gaining information and understanding, and that is entertainment. However, this book will not be much concerned with reading for entertainment. It is the least demanding kind of reading, and it requires the least amount of effort. Furthermore, there are no rules for it. Everyone who knows how to read at all can read for entertainment if he wants to.

But Richard Rodriguez's story makes me wonder if this is true. It seems to me that it is not so hard to absorb, and early in life, the idea that reading is so good for you, so loaded with vitamin-rich, high-fiber information and understanding, that it can't possibly be pleasurable—that to read for the joy of it is fundamentally inappropriate.

That Adler and Van Doren have these suspicions is indicated by their choice of the word *entertainment*—a dismissive word in comparison to ones I have just used, *pleasure* and *joy*, and often prefaced by the adjective "mere." Graham Greene wrote works of fiction that he felt were seriously literary, and called them "novels"; others, largely thrillers like *Stamboul Train* and *Brighton Rock*, he called "entertainments." But "pleasure" and "joy" are richer words, with a greater range of connotations: there can be guilty pleasures, but abiding ones as well. Adler and Van Doren don't want to get into these complications, preferring the simple distinction between entertainment, on the one trivial hand, and information and understanding, on the strong and noble other. But to divide the world of reading in this way is to leave yourself unable to account for pleasure, and likely to mistrust it when it comes.

So this is what I say to my petitioners: for heaven's sake, don't turn reading into the intellectual equivalent of eating organic greens, or (shifting the metaphor slightly) some fearfully disciplined appointment with an elliptical trainer of the mind in which you count words or pages the way some people fix their attention on the "calories burned" readout—some assiduous and taxing exercise that allows you to look back on your conquest of *Middlemarch* with grim satisfaction. How depressing. This kind of thing is not reading at all, but what C. S. Lewis once called "social and ethical hygiene."

In Lewis's view, which I largely share, the tendency to think of reading in these terms arises when critics, especially members of what Lewis called "the Vigilant school," convince others that they are the proper guardians of reading and the proper judges of what kind of reading counts. When Lewis wrote those words, the leading Vigilant Critic in England was Lewis's fellow Cambridge don, F. R. Leavis; in my place and time, no one is more Vigilant than Harold Bloom.

Some years back Bloom wrote a book called *How to Read and Why*, but it really should have been called *What to Read and What to Think about It*. It consists of many short chapters on novels, stories, and poems that belong to the Bloomian canon, chapters in which Bloom simply tells you what's important about each work and what, in general terms, it means. Though there are a few brief sections of "summary observations" in which Bloom gives some supposedly practical advice, the advice of the book as a whole is simply "Do as I say and do as I do."

Bloom has little patience for those who would expend their reading energy on non-masterpieces. If he does not have his own version of the Catholic Church's Index of Prohibited Books, he can certainly sound like he does. Consider this: in 2003 he wrote that there are only four active American writers who "deserve our praise": Philip Roth, Thomas Pynchon, Cormac McCarthy, and Don DeLillo. Of course, Bloom doesn't actually suggest that less excellent writers should be forbidden—only that we're wasting our time by reading them. (This does raise an interesting question: why does Bloom include a chapter on Tony Morrison's *Song of Solomon* in *How to Read and Why*? Surely she does not deserve such an honor, by his own reckoning of today's American novelists. And indeed, while he agrees that Morrison has certain talents, he does not straightforwardly celebrate any of her books—only saying that he prefers *Song of Solomon* to *Beloved*—and assesses her career thus: "she is very much at work, and so I will venture no prophecy as to her final eminence." Coy fellow!)

By way of illustration, we might reflect on Bloom's notorious agonies about the popularity of Harry Potter. On this subject

Bloom is not perfectly rational: for instance, he writes of his first encounter with J. K. Rowling, "As I read, I noticed that every time a character went for a walk, the author wrote instead that the character 'stretched his legs.' I began marking on the back of an envelope every time that phrase was repeated. I stopped only after I had marked the envelope several dozen times." Now, how many dozen would be "several dozen"? Four at least, I would think. So Bloom is telling us that he counted fifty or more instances of the phrase "stretched his legs" in some unspecified part (half? two-thirds?) of *Harry Potter and the Sorcerer's Stone*. This would require, not incidentally, that the book contain more than fifty instances of characters taking walks. But I will say no more, except to encourage the reader to make her own count, and to suggest that discounting Bloom's tally by a factor of twenty might bring us closer to the mark.

Some among the ancient Athenians divided human beings into two groups, those who possess *arete*—virtue, excellence—and those who don't, with the latter being fit for mockery or even slavery. When he makes proclamations about reading, Bloom can sound rather Athenian. He straightforwardly doubts that people who read Harry Potter will be willing to, or could be made to, read anything else. "A host are reading it who simply will not read superior fare, such as Kenneth Grahame's *The Wind in the Willows* or the 'Alice' books of Lewis Carroll." And in another context: "Harry Potter will not lead our children on to Kipling's *Just So Stories* or his *Jungle Book*. It will not lead them to Thurber's *Thirteen Clocks* or Kenneth Grahame's *Wind in the Willows* or Lewis Carroll's 'Alice.'" This is nothing if not definitive and is therefore of a piece with his comment (to *Newsweek* magazine in 2007) about the enormous sales of the Potter series: "I know of no larger indictment of the world's descent into subliteracy."

Bloom uses the term "subliteracy" seriously: he doubts whether people who read the Harry Potter books are actually reading *at all*. Rowling's readers are "nonreaders," and the primary benefit they derive from her books is to be "momentarily emancipated from their screens," so that they "may not forget wholly the sensation of turning the pages of a book, any book." But what good does that do, if they will never go on to "superior fare"? "Presumably, if you cannot be persuaded to read anything better, Rowling will have to do"—but, really, "Is there any redeeming educational use to Rowling? . . . Why read, if what you read will not enrich mind or spirit or personality?" Indeed: why not just stick with the screens?—if that's all you're good for. If you lack *arete*.

Bloom emphasized this point in an interview with Ray Suarez, in August 2000, on the NewsHour with Jim Lehrer. When Suarez commented, "So you have no truck with those who say, 'well, at least they're reading,' whether speaking of adults or children," Bloom replied, "Ray, they're not really. Their eyes are passing over a page. They are turning the page. Their minds are being numbed by cliché. No demands are being made upon them. Nothing . . . Nothing is happening to them. They're being schooled in what you might call unreality or the avoidance of reality."

A recent story in the *Washington Post* quotes a professor named Eric Williamson who declares of his students, "There is nary a student in the classroom—and this goes for English majors, too—who wouldn't pronounce Stephen King a better author than Donald Barthelme or William Vollmann. The students do not have any shame about reading inferior texts." Let's leave aside the question of whether Stephen King *is* a poorer writer than Barthelme or Vollmann (I wonder if Professor Williamson has ever actually made a case for his verdict in this matter) and simply ask whether we want people to read Barthelme or Vollmann or anyone else out of a sense of *shame*—not because they are intrigued by *The Dead Father* or think that *Rising Up and Rising Down* is urgent and powerful, but because they want to be seen holding such books and would be humiliated if Professor Williamson caught them with a copy of *Cujo* in hand. There's much more wisdom in a statement by the magnificently snobby and elitist critic Dwight Macdonald (1906–1982), who called himself a "conservative anarchist" and once commented, "Well, I say, being an anarchist, that I don't believe in taking people by the hand and force-feeding them culture. I think they should make their own decisions. If they want to go to museums and concerts, that's fine, but they shouldn't be seduced into doing it or shamed into doing it."

There are, it seems to me, only two possible effects that Bloom's approach can have upon readers: it can make them self-congratulatory—"Yes, I, and a few others like me, read the *proper* works"—or it can terrify them—"How can I be worthy of this high calling?" Neither response has anything to do with genuine reading. Thus Lewis, Bloom's polar opposite in this matter, imagines a group of educated adults, having been well instructed by the Vigilants, complacently discussing their recent reading; "Yet, while this goes on downstairs, the only real literary experience in such a family may be occurring in a back bedroom where a small boy is reading *Treasure Island*"—or, perhaps, Harry Potter—"under the bedclothes by the light of an electric torch."

Now, I must admit that there's a message worth noting from the other side of the readerly street. James Murphy, the lead singer for the band LCD Soundsystem, has this to say about his own reading experiences: "I actually want to write a treatise in defence of pretension. . . . I think the word pretension has become like the word ironic—just this catch-all term to distance people from interesting experiences and cultural

engagement and possible embarrassment. Pretension can lead
to other things. You know, the first time I read *Gravity's Rainbow*,
I did so because I thought it would make me seem cool. That
was my original motivation. But now I've read it six times, and
I find it hilarious and great and I understand it. You can't be
afraid to embarrass yourself sometimes." Young people often
signal through their pretensions what they hope to become: they
have discerned, maybe in a limited way, some good and they
are pursuing it as best they can, given limited knowledge and
experience. They see people whom they admire, or are in some
way attracted to, and they try to copy the preferences of those
paragons. Such copying can lead to more and more pretension;
but in many cases the pretense becomes real: the tastes we aspire
to often become our own tastes. (For better or worse: this happens with whiskey, cigarettes, drugs, and sweetbreads, as well
as books, with wildly variable results.) That achievement comes
by imitation is true, and importantly true. "Pretension can lead
to other things" is a wise word. But it is also true that we need
eventually to grow out of reliance on signaling. What is forgiv-
able and even touching in the young Richard Rodriguez can be
unpleasant in a mature adult.

And the child who reads with a pure enthusiasm, signaling
nothing to anyone, is beautiful: thus Lewis's celebration of reading unsophisticated books. Lewis's predecessor in such thoughts
was G. K. Chesterton, in his defense of the "penny dreadfuls" so
popular in the late Victorian world. "There is no class of vulgar
publications about which there is, to my mind, more utterly
ridiculous exaggeration and misconception than the current
boys' literature of the lowest stratum." Chesterton is perfectly
happy to acknowledge that these books are not in the commen-
datory sense "literature" because "the simple need for some kind
of ideal world in which fictitious persons play an unhampered

part is infinitely deeper and older than the rules of good art, and much more important. Every one of us in childhood has constructed such an invisible *dramatis personae*, but it never occurred to our nurses to correct the composition by careful comparison with Balzac."

While I agree with Harold Bloom about many things and am thankful for his long advocacy for the greatest of stories and poems, in these matters I am firmly on the side of Lewis and Chesterton. Read what gives you delight—at least most of the time—and do so without shame. And even if you are that rare sort of person who is delighted chiefly by what some people call Great Books, don't make them your steady intellectual diet, any more than you would eat at the most elegant of restaurants every day. It would be too much. Great books are great in part because of what they ask of their readers: they are not readily encountered, easily assessed. The poet W. H. Auden once wrote, "When one thinks of the attention that a great poem demands, there is something frivolous about the notion of spending every day with one. Masterpieces should be kept for High Holidays of the Spirit"— for our own personal Christmases and Easters, not for any old Wednesday.

It's noteworthy that what someone like the young Richard Rodriguez thought of as true and high seriousness—reading masterpieces and masterpieces only—Auden sees as "frivolous." This is not so paradoxical as it seems. What's frivolous is not the masterpiece itself, but the idea that at any given time I the reader am prepared to meet its standards, to rise to its challenges. Those challenges wear heavily upon the unprepared reader (at age ten or twenty or sixty) and as a result the reading, which in anticipation promised such riches of meaning, proves in fact to be that dread appointment with the elliptical trainer I mentioned earlier. And who needs that?

At the end of his memoir *Lost in the Meritocracy: The Undereducation of an Overachiever*, Walter Kirn recalls a time when, as a recent graduate of Princeton, he read a book. All his life he had read only to impress others, primarily his teachers: he had been a kind of cynical doppelgänger of Richard Rodriguez, seeing reading only as an instrument by which some other kind of good might be achieved. ("I relied on my gift for mimicking authority figures and playing back to them their own ideas as though they were conclusions I'd reached myself.... What was learning but a form of borrowing? And what was intelligence but borrowing slyly?") But having succeeded at this game, he discerns its emptiness, and the unraveling of all his ambitions leads to a near-complete breakdown: "My education was running in reverse as my mind shed its outermost layer of signs and symbols and shrank back to its dumb, preliterate state." But it's at this moment, with no one ordering him or expecting him to do any such thing, he randomly picks up and decides to read *The Adventures of Huckleberry Finn*. Then he moves on to *Great Expectations*.

> And so, belatedly, haltingly, accidentally, and quite implausibly
> and incredibly, it began at last: my education. I wasn't sure what
> it would get me, whose approval it might win, or how long it
> might take to complete (forever, I had an inkling), but for once
> those weren't my first concerns. Alone in my room, congested and
> exhausted, I forgot my obsession with self-advancement. I wanted
> to lose myself. I wanted to read. Instead of filling in the blanks,
> I wanted to be a blank and be filled in.

He concludes, "I wanted to find out what others thought." For the first time in his life, Walter Kirn was reading at whim.

And it's never too late to begin this new life as a free reader. Not long after Kirn's book came out, Cathleen Schine wrote a wonderful essay for the *New York Times* about being a "teenage

illiterate"—that is, having been turned off reading, especially literary reading, as a teenager and coming back to it only as an adult.
At one point, frustrated with her inability to find books she liked
and to stick with them, "I remembered a bag in the closet with
stuff my ex-boyfriend had left behind, including a paperback copy
of *Our Mutual Friend*, his favorite novel. A few days later I emerged
from that exquisite book and cursed myself for wasting so much of
my life doing things other than what God in all his wisdom clearly
meant for me to do for the rest of my life: read Dickens." For
Schine this discovery "was a defining moment," and "it could never
have happened if I had not been blessedly illiterate."

That is to say, she came upon a world of wonderful books when
she was ready for them—when she could receive what they have
to offer. "I got to read *Huckleberry Finn* for the first time when I was
35 years old. I read *My Antonia* for the first time *last month*. That is
a kind of grace. If . . . I had read *Huckleberry Finn* at 14, would I have
reread it at 35? Maybe, but it wouldn't have been the same tran-
scendent experience as discovering it as an adult."

So the books are waiting. Of this you may be confident: they'll
be ready when the whim strikes you.

All in your head   ☞ What's odd, when you think about it,
is that people can be seized by the whim to read in the first place.
It's not exactly a natural thing to do. As Steven Pinker once
noted, "Language is a human instinct, but written language is
not. . . . When children are thrown together without a usable language, they invent one of their own." But as for writing, "A group
of children is no more likely to invent an alphabet than to invent
the internal combustion engine. Children are wired for sound, but
print is an optional accessory that must be painstakingly bolted
on." Yet once the ability to make sense of printed words gets

itself so bolted, reading can become a deeply pleasurable activity. And it is not easy to say why.

This is a large question with many subsets. Some years ago the English critic A. D. Nuttall wrote a thoughtful book called *Why Does Tragedy Give Pleasure?* in which he explored a puzzle that people have been worrying about at least since Aristotle. One would not think that it could possibly be agreeable to watch Oedipus staggering eyeless across the stage, nor Hamlet dying from Laertes's poisoned rapier, nor Hedda Gabler rushing from her sitting room with a loaded pistol in her hand—and perhaps "agreeable" isn't really the word—nor "pleasurable"—and yet these are experiences that many intelligent and decent and even quite kind people seek out, over and over again. Curious; and yet what is perhaps more curious is that many of the same people who will go to the theater to see such horrific events will also absorb themselves in books that tell such stories and find themselves so moved that their tears drop onto the pages.

When you flip the coin of genre to the other side, the question becomes still more insistent: few of us have asked why people would want to go to the theater to see a comedy played out—laughter is always needful, and in short supply—but why might someone seek that laughter through the curious means of scanning black marks on bound pieces of paper? Is it not passing strange that a person gazing at such marks can be incapacitated by laughter? Yet most of us have had that happen to us, and almost all of us have seen it happen to others. Few things could be more mundane.

Cognitive scientists have made much progress in recent years in their attempts to understand how reading works—how it happens in the brain. A number of recent books have described this research, most notable among them Maryanne Wolf's *Proust and the Squid* and Stanislas Dehaene's *Reading in the Brain*, and their account goes something like this:

"The tale of reading," Dehaene writes, "begins when the retina receives photons reflected off the written page. But the retina is not a homogeneous sensor. Only its central part, called the fovea, is dense in high-resolution cells sensitive to incoming light, while the rest of the retina has a coarser resolution. The fovea, which occupies about 15 degrees of the visual field, is the only part of the retina that is genuinely useful for reading." This limited field of high-resolution sensing means that our eyes have to travel across a page in a series of zig-zag movements called saccades, which, once we have become experienced readers, allow us to identify words even when we just discern some of the letters in them, and sentences even when we can only truly see a couple of words at a time. We are, however, usually aware in a general way of a dozen or so letters ahead of the one we're focused on at any given time, and about 10 percent of the time our eyes are darting back over words we've already read to make sure we got them right. This rather complicated optical dance—or rather, the limited sensorial equipment that mandates the dance—places a pretty firm limit on our maximum reading speed. Fluent readers achieve about five hundred words a minute, and that's not far from the best we can do, given the limited focal abilities our retinas possess.

Our brains, however, can process words much faster than our eyes can* and are extremely skilled at filtering out noise and

---

*As Dehaene points out in a passage that I find simultaneously exciting and creepy, if we could be freed from the limitations of our eyes' sensing abilities we could achieve genuine speed-reading. "If a full sentence is presented, word by word, at the precise point where gaze is focalized, thus avoiding the need for eye movements, a good reader can read at staggering speed—a mean of eleven hundred words per minute, and up to sixteen hundred words per minute for the best readers, which is about one word every forty milliseconds and three to four times faster than normal reading! With this method, called rapid sequential visual presentation, or RSVP, identification and

discerning signals. Consider, for instance, with what apparent effortlessness we can identify a word—any old word, for instance, "reading"—whether it is presented to us in lowercase or uppercase, even though most of the letters in "READING" look quite different in the two cases. Nor do we have any trouble recognizing the same word when it is laboriously printed by young Jason or written in an elegant Palmer hand by Aunt Bess.

The almost frictionless processing of this information takes place mostly in a particular region of the brain: Dehaene says we can find it "on the edge of the left occipito-temporal fissure," and I'll have to take his word for that. The really astonishing thing, though, is that this very location is where you can find readers' brains doing the heavy lifting of decoding written words, whether those words are written in English, Hebrew, or Chinese—that is, whether you're reading from left to right or right to left, whether your language is alphabetic or (partially) ideographic. None of those distinctions matters to the text-processing brain. Nor does it matter how you learn to read, whether through phonics or a whole-language approach or any other method. Japanese readers have to navigate three completely different systems of notation, Kanji and two varieties of Kana, katakana and hiragana, which can show up within one text, for instance in a newspaper—and they use the same general region of the brain in each case. As Dehaene says, it really looks "as though there were a cerebral organ for reading," though there is not: there has not been sufficient evolutionary time for one to develop, since humans have been reading

---

comprehension remain satisfactory, thus suggesting that the duration of those central steps does not impose a strong constraint on normal reading. Perhaps this computerized presentation mode represents the future of reading in a world where screens progressively replace paper."

for just a few thousand years and evolutionary change moves at a much slower rate. How there can be such uniformity of brain function without biological evolution directly supporting it is something that Dehaene explains in detail and with great clarity; but we need not get into that here.

Both Dehaene and Wolf are particularly interested in how the smoothness and ease of reading can be disrupted, by accident or disease, and in how some people are never able to achieve fluent reading. This emphasis makes sense for two reasons. First, dysfunction is often the biological researcher's best guide to proper function: if you can pinpoint what causes a mechanism to go wrong, you usually learn a good deal about what has to be in place for it to go right. As Dehaene explains, some of the most important early research into the cognitive contexts of reading came when a nineteenth-century Frenchman, known in the literature as Monsieur C, woke up one morning and found himself unable to read. He could still speak perfectly well, could write fluently, and could even recognize written numbers—but he could not read at all. When it was discovered that he had had a stroke, and that the stroke had left disabling lesions in a particular part of his brain, the scientists observing Monsieur C were able to conclude that the ability to read was associated with a different part of the brain than the ability to write, speak, and discern numbers.

Second, the kind of research Dehaene and Wolf do is most practically beneficial to people, especially children, who have reading difficulties. Wolf is actually a professor of child development, and both she and Dehaene have much to say about dyslexia and related disorders. Both of them hope that their work can aid those who seek to treat dyslexia, and also that it will have an effect on teachers' ways of teaching reading to young children. Dehaene even allows himself a few moments of (justifiable) annoyance at the way that "childhood reading experts" continue their debates about the best strategies for teaching reading to children in complete ignorance of a large and growing body of work on how the human brain processes written language.

All of this is, to me anyway, abidingly fascinating, and yet, as I explore these books, there's a part of me that's always saying "But you're not really talking about *reading*"—about whatever it is that makes me cackle and snort when I have a P. G. Wodehouse novel in my hands, even when I'm in bed and desperately trying to stifle the laughter lest I wake my wife up, which I always end up doing anyway, with the result that for some years now I have been forbidden to bring a Wodehouse book to bed. Or whatever it is about the last scenes of *King Lear* that grieved the young Samuel Johnson so terribly that he simply had to set the play aside for decades. ("I might relate," he wrote in his magisterial edition of Shakespeare, "that I was many years ago so shocked by Cordelia's death, that I know not whether I ever endured to read again the last scenes of the play till I undertook to revise them as an editor.") Or, for that matter, that terrible moment when Tolstoy's Anna Karenina, on a long railway journey, becomes so involved in the exciting life of a character in a novel that, wanting such excitement for herself, she becomes helpless to resist the temptations of adultery (to which she was already vulnerable). Surely those experiences are what reading is all about.

Such a response is largely unfair to Wolf and Dehaene. Of course they are talking about reading—just a different aspect of reading than I am habitually interested in. Their concern might be summed up in this passage from Dehaene: "A written text is not a high-fidelity recording. Its goal is not to reproduce speech as we pronounce it, but rather to code it at a level abstract enough to allow the reader to quickly retrieve its meaning." At the purely

cognitive level, this is what reading is: coding and decoding. It
is a communications system, deeply similar to what a computer
does when it decodes the zeroes and ones of a program, or what
happens when, as our cells reproduce, strands of DNA are read
and copied. Reading in this sense is accessible by some variety of
information theory; and reading in this sense is a titanically important object of study. But reading in this sense is not the subject of
this book.

I found that when I encountered Wolf's and especially
Dehaene's accounts of these physiological processes, I was nearly
disabled as a reader. I kept thinking about the movements of my
eyes, and it's not possible to be so self-conscious and still make
sense of a text. I had to go over some passages multiple times,
making very deliberate efforts not to think about what I was doing.
(The experience reminded me of times when, while descend-
ing stairs rapidly, I suddenly become aware of my legs' movements, my body's balance—and immediately have to slow down
to a senior citizen's pace.) Perhaps you, gentle reader, are having
similar issues as you read this section? Such disruptions serve as
a reminder of what a strange and wonderful thing the everyday
experience of reading really is.

In a justly famous passage in Dickens's *David Copperfield*, young
David is trying to adjust to his dreary life with the rigid, humor-
less, and probably malicious Murdstone family. "As to any recre-
ation with other children of my age, I had very little of that; for
the gloomy theology of the Murdstones made all children out
to be a swarm of little vipers (though there was a child once set
in the midst of the Disciples), and held that they contaminated
one another. The natural result of this treatment . . . was to make
me sullen, dull, and dogged." Natural indeed. "I believe I should
have been almost stupefied," David continues, "but for one
circumstance."

It was this. My father had left a small collection of books in a little room upstairs, to which I had access (for it adjoined my own) and which nobody else in our house ever troubled. From that blessed little room, Roderick Random, Peregrine Pickle, Humphrey Clinker, Tom Jones, the Vicar of Wakefield, Don Quixote, Gil Blas, and Robinson Crusoe, came out, a glorious host, to keep me company. They kept alive my fancy, and my hope of something beyond that place and time,—they, and the Arabian Nights, and the Tales of the Genii,—and did me no harm; for whatever harm was in some of them was not there for me; I knew nothing of it. . . . It is curious to me how I could ever have consoled myself under my small troubles (which were great troubles to me), by impersonating my favourite characters in them—as I did—and by putting Mr. and Miss Murdstone into all the bad ones—which I did too. I have been Tom Jones (a child's Tom Jones, a harmless creature) for a week together. I have sustained my own idea of Roderick Random for a month at a stretch, I verily believe.*

"This was my only and my constant comfort," David concludes. "When I think of it, the picture always rises in my mind, of a summer evening, the boys at play in the churchyard, and I sitting on my bed, reading as if for life."

---

*The characters David refers to are the protagonists of popular novels of adventure, largely from the eighteenth century. The first three names are the eponymous heroes of books by Tobias Smollett; then come Henry Fielding's *Tom Jones* and Oliver Goldsmith's *Vicar of Wakefield*, followed by Cervantes's *Don Quixote* (the one pre-1700 book on the list); *Gil Blas* is a French novel by Alain-René Lesage that was influenced by Cervantes and in turn deeply influenced Smollett; and everyone knows Defoe's *Robinson Crusoe*. Although many of these books are now considered classics, in their day they were thought of as something close to "penny dreadfuls": light and frivolous reading, often denounced from pulpits as being injurious to good morals.

Reading as if for life—how does this happen? At this point
I cannot stress too much that I do not raise the spirit of David
Copperfield as a means of denouncing the research of Wolf and
Dehaene, as a means of celebrating the angelic Humanities at the
expense of that beast Science. Such a move would be cheap, silly,
and wrong. Rather, I simply want to emphasize that, having better
understood the near-miracle of our ability to decode marks on
paper, we are left with a truth equally remarkable: that some of
us greatly *desire* to do so, and that some of us find abiding consolation in what we encounter when our eyes scan words on the page
in those strange jerky saccades. That images striking the retina can
be transferred to the edge of the left occipito-temporal fissure,
and there can be decoded, is extraordinary; that what is decoded
there can bring tears to the eyes, or cause laughter to rise up from
the diaphragm, or bring to a deeply unhappy boy cut off from his
beloved mother a few hours, or many hours, of joy . . . I don't have
words to express how deeply strange this is. I encouraged you in
my previous section to "read at whim!"—but why would anyone
ever be struck by that particular whim? This is a mystery.

Aspirations   ⌒ Some readers may be puzzled to find that this
book didn't end several pages ago. *Read at whim*, I told you—What
more is there to say?

Perhaps there's a little more that could be said. "Whim" may not
cover *all* the bases. But before I go any further I want to insist that
it remains the foundation. It should be normal for us to read what
we want to read, to read what we truly enjoy reading. However,
even if we follow that model, there will be times when we ask,
along with the old song, "Is that all there is?" We may well wonder
if there are other books—or other kinds of books than the ones we
typically prefer—that might give us pleasure or edification or both.

Children often have this experience: the Harry Potter saga has wrapped up, the Anne of Green Gables tales are done. Neil Gaiman, that gifted writer of fantasies for children and adults, gave a talk a few years ago in which he described the centrality of C. S. Lewis's Narnia books to his early life: "I remember what I did on my seventh birthday—I lay on my bed and I read the books all through, from the first to the last. For the next four or five years I continued to read them. I would read other books, of course, but in my heart I knew that I read them only because there wasn't an infinite number of Narnia books to read." It's no wonder that writers besiege C. S. Lewis's estate seeking permission to write further Narnian adventures, or that responsibility for Nancy Drew and the Hardy Boys has been passed on to several generations of authors, who will continue to invent new mysteries for the young sleuths to unravel probably until the world's end.

But adults can feel the same grief: how many thousands of readers have never been able to reconcile themselves to the fact that Jane Austen wrote only six novels? Thus the recent sequels to *Pride and Prejudice*—even, in a perverse way, *Pride and Prejudice and Zombies*—and the attempts by various authors to complete the novels Austen was working on when she died. A similar speculative eagerness surrounds Dickens's unfinished *Mystery of Edward Drood*: Why did Dickens have to die at fifty-eight? Surely he had not only this novel but half-a-dozen more in him!

So we return again and again to our favorites, striving to calculate how best to maintain the magic. I have had several conversations with my son over the years at moments when he was undecided whether his last encounter with the Harry Potter books had receded sufficiently in his memory that a successful rereading was possible. And success in such endeavors is a doubtful thing: there is always the possibility, devotees know all too well, that too many rereadings squeezed into too narrow a time frame will drain the books' power and leave them forever inert on the shelves. And this

would be lamentable. (Lately I have been asking myself whether
I have sufficiently forgotten the details of Patrick O'Brien's novels
of the Royal Navy during the Napoleonic Wars that I can return
to them with vibrant pleasure. I hover over those memories like a
cook over a stewpot: in another year, I think, the books and I will
be ready.)

So whim cannot be everything. My whim may take me to the
same books always, but I am confronted by that iron-clad Law of
Diminishing Returns. I simply *must* turn elsewhere, to seek out
alternatives, even if, like Neil Gaiman contemplating Narnia,
I know that no alternative can match the Real Thing that I most
love. So what do I do?

What some people do is make, or contribute to, Web sites. This
form of devotional practice is certainly more common among
men, which means that Tolkien gets more cyberspatial attention
than Austen, as do other world-making fantasists who follow,
in that respect, the Tolkienian model. (Austen's presence on
Wikipedia is dwarfed by that of two dozen or more fantasy and
science-fiction writers. The entries for Stephanie Meyer's Twilight
series are getting longer, but still have a ways to catch up to the
books that have a large percentage of male readers.)

There is also the "fanfic" world: sequels or continuations of
existing books written by an author's most passionate followers.
That wondrous storyteller Michael Chabon describes in an essay
his response to reading, at age ten, Arthur Conan Doyle's first
short story featuring Sherlock Holmes, "A Scandal in Bohemia."
That response was to sit down and write his own Sherlock
Holmes story. Later he read everything Conan Doyle had written about Baker Street's most prominent sleuth, but in the long
run that wasn't sufficient: when he was around forty he wrote
his own Sherlock Holmes novel, a powerful tale called *The Final
Solution*. It's easy to see why Chabon believes that "all literature,
highbrow or low, from the *Aeneid* onward, is fan fiction. That is

why Harold Bloom's notion of the anxiety of influence has always rung so hollow to me. . . . All novels are sequels; influence is bliss."

But the writing of stories in response to stories is not a gift that every reader has. And the varieties of homage I have been describing, while they may fill the time between rereadings, and indeed serve as a distinct form of rereading—since the books to be documented or imitated must regularly be consulted, as a biblical scholar writing a commentary must always have the sacred text open on the writing desk—even these creative devotional engagements will eventually pall. And the passionate reader will eventually be plopped once more in front of the question: Is that all there is?

At such times it is often tempting to seek out imitators: modern writers of Austenian romances, copycat Harrys,* epic tales that make no mention of Tolkien but include plenty of wizards, dwarves, elves, and hobbits (though under various names and with slight modifications). But that way madness lies. Or, if not madness, one of two equally unpleasant alternatives: a frustration and boredom that can lead you away from reading altogether, or a gradual acceptance of works of lower and lower quality.

The dangers of the Path of Frustration should be obvious: the world doesn't need fewer readers. But the Path of Acceptance may be still more worrisome. The readers who love *The Lord of the Rings* so much that they turn to all the Tolkien imitators—or those who love Jane Austen so much that they turn to the *Pride and Prejudice* sequels— must learn to get by with less. They must learn to accept plots less clever and surprising, characters less vivid, prose less dynamic and

---

*The further adventures of Harry, unknown to J. K. Rowling, are especially big in China, where you may find such titles as *Harry Potter and the Hiking Dragon*, *Harry Potter and the Chinese Empire*, *Harry Potter and the Young Heroes*, *Harry Potter and Leopard-Walk-Up-to-Dragon*, *Harry Potter and the Big Funnel*, and *Harry Potter and the Waterproof Pearl*.

precise, thoughts less insightful and wise. They place themselves in
the intellectual equivalent of postwar Britain, practicing austerity
measures, presided over by a kind of internal Sir Stafford Cripps.

Sir Stafford was the Chancellor of the Exchequer in those dark
years after the war, and the flamboyant and extravagant Winston
Churchill hated nothing so much as Cripps's pinched abstemious-
ness. The story is told that when Churchill was visiting North
Africa he said, "Here we are, marooned in all these miles of
sand—not one blade of grass or drop of water or a flower. How
Cripps would love it." A joke, of course, and yet beneath the joke
a warning that a necessary austerity can become, for some, a
preferred condition. Similarly, once a reader is acclimated to the
pedestrian, the mundane, and the predictable, he or she can come to
accept them as normal—normal, if not delightful.

Now, in making this point, have I not reinstated the dominance
of the Vigilant School that I deplored in the previous section?
Am I not echoing Harold Bloom's denunciations of the literarily
insufficient? Not at all, for the authority I would appeal to here is
not some culturally sanctioned (or self-sanctioned) critical arbiter,
or even the kind of strictness of readerly conscience that drove
Richard Rodriguez through every last page of Plato's *Republic*. On
the other hand, I think Bloom is right to reject the too-easy and
often-recited "at least they're reading" trope—wrong when he says
that reading Harry Potter books has zero value and isn't reading at
all, but right when he scorns the idea that the act of passing one's
eyes over a page is so intrinsically valuable that it doesn't matter
what words the eyes are scanning.[*]

---

[*] On this matter the writer Alex Rose makes a wickedly good point: "The only
conceivable value of trashy books is the dubious but not unthinkable possibility that they
might go some of the way towards engendering in young people a love of reading as an

So if I don't want to say that all reading is equally good, equally valuable, but I also don't want to give in to the Vigilant School, then what standard of readerly value am I appealing to? Answer: I am appealing to the standard of the reader's own pleasure—a criterion that sounds more simple and straightforward than it is.

Consider the case of Edward Gibbon, of *Decline and Fall of the Roman Empire* fame. He became one of the most celebrated of all historians, but his intellectual beginnings were not auspicious. At the age of fourteen, he was sent by his father to Oxford at a time (the mid-eighteenth century) when that university had virtually forgotten its intellectual and pedagogical calling; he would later write that the time he spent at Magdalen College was "the most idle and unprofitable of my whole life."

Even my childish reading had displayed an early though blind propensity for books; and the shallow flood might have been taught to flow in a deep channel and a clear stream. In the discipline of a well-constituted academy, under the guidance of skilful and vigilant professors, I should gradually have risen from translations to originals, from the Latin to the Greek classics, from dead languages to living science: my hours would have been occupied by useful and agreeable studies, the wanderings of fancy would have been restrained, and I should have

---

end in-itself, which in turn might whet the appetite for better books. For many, that's the only way in. They'll read *Sweet Valley High* or *Twilight* at thirteen, lose their taste for it by fourteen and demand something richer and more challenging at sixteen. Or so the thinking goes.

If the argument applies to one form of entertainment, though, it should apply to all. Why is it that when kids become enraptured by some idiotic program, no one says, 'Well, at least they're watching TV?' "

escaped the temptations of idleness, which finally precipitated my departure from Oxford.

(Gibbon is utterly withering about the Oxford faculty of the time, whom he sardonically refers to as "monks" because of the monastic origins of the university: "The fellows or monks of my time were decent easy men, who supinely enjoyed the gifts of the founder; their days were filled by a series of uniform employments; the chapel and the hall, the coffee-house and the common room, till they retired, weary and well satisfied, to a long slumber. From the toil of reading, or thinking, or writing, they had absolved their conscience; and the first shoots of learning and ingenuity withered on the ground, without yielding any fruits to the owners or the public.")

Gibbon soon learned that the "monk" assigned to be his tutor was about as "supine" as the others and would not be the source of any significant instruction. Eventually the boy decided to skip a tutorial, and when he discovered that his abject apology was readily and unquestioningly accepted, made skipping the norm rather than the exception. When this tutor left the university, he was replaced by one who was still less responsible: "Dr. _____ well remembered that he had a salary to receive, and only forgot that he had a duty to perform." This malign neglect left an extraordinarily gifted but lazy and undisciplined boy to his own devices—to, let us be honest, his own whims. And those whims, he later came to believe, were not kind to him.

Such a result cannot be surprising to anyone who has spent time around adolescent boys, even gifted ones; but there are lessons here for all of us. The chief one is this: Gibbon's completely unregulated and undisciplined life *made him miserable*. His father may have been ashamed of him; Oxford may have inflicted stern judgment upon him; but these are not his complaints. When he

looks back he thinks that with even limited intellectual direction, his "hours would have been occupied by useful and agreeable
studies"—*agreeable* being the key word here. Had he had legitimate
work to do, challenging work to do, he would have been happier.
That he also would have been more pleasing to his father and the
President of Magdalen is surely true and equally surely irrelevant.

Because Gibbon had neither external nor internal direction,
he floundered. He read almost nothing while he was resident at
Magdalen, chiefly because he had a strong sense of confinement
in that (to him) monastic space, and since his "chief pleasure was
that of travelling," he got out of town whenever possible. Interestingly, during the holidays, when he was back home, he did not feel
so confined and his love of reading returned. But he was guided
only by "a blind propensity for books," a "blind and boyish taste for
the pursuit of exotic history"—and his books, like those sequels
to *Pride and Prejudice* and ersatz Harry Potters, began to lose their
savor. Why, then, bother to read at all?

Idleness eventually led Gibbon in an odd direction: toward
religious, or maybe it would be better to say ecclesiastical, enthusiasm. He decided to be received into the Catholic Church, which
led his father to yank him out of England altogether and place
him in the charge of a good Swiss Protestant. It was under the
unexpectedly tender and sensitive care of this man that Gibbon
first began to pursue the life of the mind in a serious way. So he
eventually received some helpful direction, genuine guidance that
did not refute or replace his innate preferences but helped him to
see where those preferences properly led. The boy who had blindly
pursued "exotic history" became a man whose masterpiece is just
that: a comprehensive and brilliantly related account of the exotic
worlds of ancient Rome and medieval Constantinople.

It might be thought that Gibbon's story is not especially
relevant to the reader of this book, who is likely to be out of

school and unlikely to find a kindly Swiss Protestant to become his or her instructor. What does Edward Gibbon's dissolute adolescence have to do with us? But I think Gibbon's experience is immensely relevant. It helps us to make a vital distinction between what I shall call *whim* and *Whim*. In its lower-case version, whim is thoughtless, directionless preference that almost invariably leads to boredom or frustration or both. But Whim is something very different: it can guide us because it is based in self-knowledge—it can become for us a gracious Swiss pedagogue of the mind.

Let's recall the man whose reading habits prompted Randall Jarrell to coin the phrase that we have been using, the man who read and reread Kipling's *Kim* "not to teach, not to criticize, just for love—he read it, as Kipling wrote it, just because he liked to, wanted to, couldn't help himself." Interestingly, the man was a *critic*—a person who read and thought about and wrote about books for a living, who had the discernment to grasp a key point: that he was going to kill himself as a reader if he did not allow himself the right and privilege of returning, from time to time, as Whim took him, to something that gave him nothing but pleasure. A book he would never, ever write a word about. What moved him was not whim but Whim, because he knew himself, knew what he needed, knew what would give him the kind of delight that he craved. I think Jarrell has this in mind when he says that this kind of reading, if only "during the contemplative and sympathetic hours of our reading," "is surely within our power, if we choose to make it so, if we choose to let one part of our nature follow its natural desires." *One part of our nature*: the part that knows itself and therefore seeks what is really good.

The better we know ourselves the better we will be able to make some of the decisions that all readers must face—for instance, and notably, the decision to persist in reading a book that fails to delight. For the young Richard Rodriguez, and for anyone else who is reading in order to get through a list, this question does not arise: enjoyment, or the lack thereof, has no bearing on the task. A dentist filling a tooth doesn't stop because the task brings no pleasure; nor on this account does the truly diligent reader. But the rest of us are faced with choices, and if we're reading for our own pleasure the choices are especially complex. For if this particular book is not giving me pleasure *now*, it may give me pleasure *later*, if I allow it to do so. Maybe it's just starting slowly but will pick up speed; maybe I haven't fully grasped the idiom it's working in but eventually will figure it out; maybe the problem is not with the book but with my own powers of concentration because I slept fitfully last night. Or maybe, for some reason I don't understand, today is not one of the High Holidays of my spirit.

Many maybes. But in any case, I have to decide whether to persevere, and for a long time my default position was to continue. Indeed, I was twenty years old before I failed to finish a book I had started: it was *The Recognitions*, a novel by William Gaddis, and I gave up, after an extended period of moral paralysis, at page 666. That day I grieved, feeling that I had been forced from some noble pedestal; but I woke up the next morning with my soul singing. After all, though I would never get back the hours I had devoted to those 666 pages, the hours I *would have spent* ploughing through the remaining four hundred were mine to spend as I would. I had been granted time as a pure and sweet gift.

Of course, once you have abandoned a book after more than six hundred pages, abandoning one after fifty seems trivial. But for me that wasn't a bad thing. I needed to overcome the sense of duty that had marched me through so many books before the ultimately liberating, if at the time miserable, experience of *The Recognitions*; and I needed to learn, as I eventually did, that if I set a book aside today I am not thereby forbidding myself to return to it later— nor am I promising to do so. To everything there is a season, and, by corollary, everything is sometimes *out* of season. Perhaps there will even come a time for me to read *The Recognitions*. But no one will be able to tell me when that season comes; I will have to discern that for myself, with the aid of many years of reflecting on the kind of reader I am.

Those of us who want to be better readers have to be self-guided in this way. And one of the primary reasons I am so suspicious of *How to Read a Book* and similar guides is that they promise to help us offload accountability for our reading: they say, implicitly, that self-knowledge and discernment aren't needful because experts can take care of that for us. But if we reject that implicit claim, we are left with the question of how to achieve what Gibbon achieved—the move from a "blind propensity" to informed consent to Whim's sovereignty—without a teacher to direct us. This question will govern much of what I will have to say through the rest of this book

Upstream   ☞ Let us start by returning to the case of the reader as *fan*: the person who has read all the Narnia books or all of Dickens's novels, and who wonders where to turn, especially if fanfiction and professional sequels don't seem to help. One possible, and rather simple, expedient is this: we can turn our temporal attention upstream rather than downstream—toward what preceded Tolkien or Austen or whomever rather than what succeeded them. After all, Austen became the Austen we know largely through her reading—something that is true of almost all writers. (I don't want to suggest here that earlier is always better: if after reading Homer you read Virgil, and after Virgil Dante, you're not exactly slumming it. But, because our own lives move forward in time, or maybe just because we have prejudice in favor of the new, our natural tendency is to move downstream. It's a tendency worth resisting, sometimes.)

The pursuit of the works that shaped a loved writer's mind can be fascinating in itself. One of the most remarkably odd and yet enlightening books in the history of literary criticism is a thick, square tome by John Livingston Lowes called *The Road to Xanadu: A Study in the Ways of the Imagination*. The book, which was published in 1927 and in the editions I've seen runs to seven hundred pages or so, is a simple inquiry into what Samuel Taylor Coleridge read that found its way into his poem "Kubla Khan." The inventory that Lowes creates is one of the most wonderfully bizarre miscellanies imaginable. To take but one example, consider the poem's great wild fountain:

> And from this chasm, with ceaseless turmoil seething,
> As if this earth in fast thick pants were breathing,
> A mighty fountain momently was forced:
> Amid whose swift half-intermitted burst
> Huge fragments vaulted like rebounding hail,
> Or chaffy grain beneath the thresher's flail:
> And 'mid these dancing rocks at once and ever
> It flung up momently the sacred river.*

It turns out that Coleridge didn't come up with this image on his own, but rather took it from a popular book of the eighteenth century commonly called *Bartram's* Travels. William Bartram is the author, and the book's full title is *Travels through North and South Carolina, Georgia, East and West Florida, the Cherokee Country, the Extensive Territories of the Muscogulges or Creek Confederacy, and the Country of the Chactaws. Containing an Account of the Soil and Natural Productions of Those Regions; Together with Observations on the*

---

* C. S. Lewis always thought that line about the earth's "fast thick pants" pretty funny, so if you snickered at that phrase you're in learned company.

Manners of the Indians. So, it turns out, the Asiatic despot's sacred river has its origins not far from Tallahassee.

Any search for the reading-that-makes-the-writer will turn up strange tidbits of this kind, but one need not investigate such matters as minutely as Lowes does in *The Road to Xanadu* in order to discover what has shaped a particular writer's thought. Anyone who wants to have a deeper and more sympathetic understanding of Jane Austen would do well to read the Gothic romances and epistolary novels of the previous century, along with, as that outstanding critic Tony Tanner has shown, the philosophy of John Locke and David Hume. One of Hume's philosophical emphases is the power of what he calls "impressions," and once you know what Hume means by that word it becomes really interesting to note that the original title of *Pride and Prejudice* was *First Impressions*.

Similarly, if you want to understand Tolkien better you might want to start by reading *Beowulf*, and some of the Eddas and sagas of medieval Iceland, and then perhaps *Sir Gawain and the Green Knight*; and it would even be worthwhile to get to know the nineteenth-century medievalism that Tolkien despised and against which he reacted, or thought he reacted. Listening to the music of Wagner would help also.*

Kipling's commendation of old books is a wise one and good to recall in this context:

If we pay no attention to words whatever, we may become like the isolated gentleman who invents a new perpetual-motion machine on old lines in ignorance of all previous plans, and then is

---

* Of course, anyone who really wants to get near the bottom of the mystery of Tolkien would need to learn Welsh and Finnish, on which he based his Elvish languages Quenya and Sindharin . . . but this is perhaps too discouraging a thought for this book, which is meant to encourage.

> surprised that it doesn't work. If we confine our attention entirely
> to the slang of the day—that is to say, if we devote ourselves
> exclusively to modern literature—we get to think the world is
> progressing when it is only repeating itself.... [I]t is only when
> one reads what men wrote long ago that one realises how abso-
> lutely modern the best of the old things are.

Beyond the buck-up-old-chap tone (the quotation comes from
a talk to teenage boys), there's a key point here: if you turn
upstream to see where your favorite authors came from, intellectually speaking, you may discover all sorts of works that are
fascinating, illuminating—but also, yes, challenging. "Challenging"
is precisely what the (downstream) imitators usually are not, but
that means that they're not all that rewarding either. They tend to
be mere shadows of the originals they strive to copy. Austen and
Tolkien weren't trying to copy anything, but they were drawing
on the power of earlier writers and thinkers, and deepening their
own sensibilities by doing so. If you imitate them in that sense—
not by trying to write what they wrote but to read what they
read—you'll find your horizons expanding, your mind stretching, your resources of knowledge coming near their limits. But
all this will draw you closer in powerful ways to the writers you
most love. That at first will be your incentive, though perhaps
as you continue the pursuit will come to have its own fascina-
tion. *Sir Gawain and the Green Knight* isn't interesting only because
Tolkien loved it: it's a brilliant and witty and subtle and harrowing
poem in its own right, a masterpiece of English poetic storytell-
ing. And reading it yields not just a better understanding of Tolkien
but a reading *experience* that resembles, that may even exceed in
power, what the Tolkien-lover had with *The Lord of the Rings*. That
is the best of all results when one is swimming up the literary
stream—to find writers and works you love even more than the

ones that prompted your adventure—but it is also, I must admit, one of the rarer ones.

And like all adventures, these have their challenges. Wise as Hume is, and instructive as his philosophy can be about not just Austen but about each of his readers, it would be useless to pretend that any modern reader can merrily skip through Hume as through a summer meadow. At the risk of damaging my case as thoroughly as I might by recommending the study of Welsh or Finnish, let me give you a little taste of the eminent Scotsman—pausing only to say that no one who loves Jane Austen *needs* to read Hume. No obligations here: we're still dwelling under the sign of Whim. But if, having learned that some of Austen's ideas about people seem to be derived, directly or indirectly, from Hume, you decided that you'd like to learn a little more about this philosophical gentleman, here's the kind of thing you'd find (quoted at some length, to give the true flavor):

All the colors of poetry, however splendid, can never paint natural objects in such a manner as to make the description be taken for a real landscape. The most lively thought is still inferior to the dullest sensation.

We may observe a like distinction to run through all the other perceptions of the mind. A man in a fit of anger, is actuated in a very different manner from one who only thinks of that emotion. If you tell me, that any person is in love, I easily understand your meaning, and from a just conception of his situation; but never can mistake that conception for the real disorders and agitations of the passion. When we reflect on our past sentiments and affections, our thought is a faithful mirror, and copies its objects truly; but the colors which it employs are faint and dull, in comparison of those in which our original perceptions were clothed.

It requires no nice discernment or metaphysical head to mark the distinction between them.

Here therefore we may divide all the perceptions of the mind into two classes or species, which are distinguished by their different degrees of force and vivacity. The less forcible and lively are commonly denominated Thoughts or Ideas. The other species want a name in our language, and in most others; I suppose, because it was not requisite for any, but philosophical purposes, to rank them under a general term or appellation. Let us, therefore, use a little freedom, and call them Impressions; employing that word in a sense somewhat different from the usual. By the term impression, then, I mean all our more lively perceptions, when we hear, or see, or feel, or love, or hate, or desire, or will. And impressions are distinguished from ideas, which are the less lively perceptions, of which we are conscious, when we reflect on any of those sensations or movements above mentioned.

Now, if you've read those paragraphs, and if you're still with me, my guess is that you will have a general sense of what Hume is talking about but you may not feel confident that you have grasped his distinctions fully. But that's to be expected, because Hume never thought we would read his work in the way we would read, say, a novel by Jane Austen.

Most of us read novels in the generally unconscious belief that we can get through them at a pretty good clip, and (this is even more important) that one good read-through is all we need to do. That eminent critic Hugh Kenner once commented that "a book— certainly, a novel—normally presupposes that ideal attention will reap it at one traverse; if we need, as we frequently do, repeated readings, that is because our attention is plagued with lapses, or perhaps because the writing is faulty." (The context of this comment, by the way, is an explanation of James Joyce's *Ulysses*,

which, Kenner justifiably claims, is designed to thwart any attempt
to "reap it in one traverse.") We don't plan to pause very often,
or to thumb back through the pages to earlier sections for clari-
fication or correction—not in the normal course of events. But
Hume expects us to be patient, to follow the development of his
ideas slowly and methodically, to pause (at the ends of paragraphs
perhaps) to make sure that we grasp his chief point before moving
on to the next one. This is not to say that Hume doesn't care about
writing clearly—in fact, he writes more than clearly: he is one of
the masters of English prose. But what he is writing about is
necessarily dense and difficult; this means that reading him is,
equally necessarily, a slow process.

For almost all of us, then, Hume's writing will provide a kind of
test—an opportunity to find out just how much patience we have,
how much time we're willing to take. And to spare any suspense
on this point, the results of that test will almost certainly be: not
patient enough. But this is no cause for discouragement. A person
who had been sedentary for a lifetime would not think that she
could rise up from her sofa, head out the door, and run a breezy
10 K. Instead she would work up to it slowly, starting with a few
strolls around the block perhaps, then longer walks, then a little
jogging, and so on. The same applies to the reading of texts written in an unfamiliar idiom or genre, or written in an age whose
stylistic preferences differ from our own.

Moreover, it's not necessary for any of us—any of us who
are not professional philosophers anyway—to work through the
whole of Hume's big book, even if (on a whim, as it were) we
pick it up at all. If we just read with care that passage I have just
excerpted, we will learn a few things about how we form our
convictions, and why we tend to hold more firmly to some than
to others. And we will, perhaps, notice that because Elizabeth
Bennett didn't know enough about Fitzwilliam Darcy to form

legitimate *ideas* about him, she instead formed only *impressions*—and such impressions once formed, as Hume teaches us, are notoriously difficult to eradicate. Elizabeth learned this the hard way, though, fortunately for her and for Mr. Darcy and for us, she ultimately discarded those impressions and replaced them with other, sounder ones. And equipped with those sounder impressions she was able to become a happy woman herself and make a worthy man equally happy. This is what sound practical philosophy can accomplish.

Some forms of intellectual labor are worth the trouble. In those times when Whim isn't quite enough, times that will come to us all, we discover this. Such work strengthens our minds, makes us more capable of concentration, teaches us patience—and almost certainly a touch of humility as well, as we struggle to navigate the difficult (if elegant) terrain of Hume's prose. But what do we have more need for, in our whirling mental worlds, than strength and concentration and patience and humility? These are virtues worth aspiring to, especially because they lead to new and greater delights.

Responsiveness   ☞ There's a justly famous passage in the letters of that great and terrible thinker Niccolo Machiavelli about reading. We are inclined to think of Machiavelli as a fierce, wily political schemer—that's what his name now means, to many of us—and so it may be surprising to hear the warmth and enthusiasm with which he describes his life as a reader:

> When evening has come, I return to my house and go into my study. At the door I take off my clothes of the day, covered with mud and mire, and I put on my regal and courtly garments; and decently reclothed, I enter the ancient courts of ancient men,

where, received by them lovingly, I feed on the food that alone
is mine and that I was born for. There I am not ashamed to speak
with them and to ask them the reason for their actions; and they in
their humanity reply to me. And for the space of four hours I feel
no boredom, I forget every pain, I do not fear poverty, death does
not frighten me.

At this time in his life—he wrote these words in 1513, when he
was forty-four years old—Machiavelli certainly knew something
about pain and fear. Earlier in that year, in the midst of one of
the political upheavals that regularly afflicted his native city of
Florence in those days, he had been removed from his position as
governor of the city's militia, charged with conspiracy against the
new government, imprisoned, tortured, beaten, and then driven
into exile. He retired to his house in the country and rediscov-
ered the pleasures of reading. Even when walking about during
the day, supervising various projects on his estate, he always had
with him a small book of poetry, Dante or Petrarch or Ovid. But
as he explains in this letter, the bulk of his reading was done in the
evenings, in what must strike us as an extraordinarily ceremonious
custom.

This is aspirational reading indeed. Machiavelli enters into
the presence of the major writers of the past as though entering the court of a great prince: thus his "regal and courtly gar-
ments." He clearly thinks that he must show himself worthy to
enjoy their company; he must be on his best behavior and must
demonstrate appropriate respect. (It's not likely that Machiavelli
would have had much sympathy with Auden's claim that "there
is something frivolous about the notion of spending every day"
with a masterpiece.) And yet these masters condescend—I use
the word in its old sense, in which the high and the mighty show
their virtue by coming down among the rest of us—these masters

condescend to welcome a disgraced government official into their company. When Machiavelli enters his study he need not be anxious about the reception he will receive, or worry that his enemies have staged a coup and overthrown his friends. He will be greeted warmly as always, because there is nothing these masters like better than the attentive company of respectful guests. For Machiavelli makes it clear that in the deepest sense he is the guest, even though in a superficial sense it is his own study he enters. The wisdom and grace to be found in that room belong more to the writers—those whom in the Middle Ages would have been called *auctors*, both authors and authorities—than to him.

Machiavelli creates a very beautiful image, but, democrats and egalitarians as we are, does his behavior not strike us as a tad obsequious?—rather too servile? And, while we're at it, do we really want to make Machiavelli, of all people, our model reader? All that time in the company of his noble intellectual predecessors didn't exactly make him into a paragon of nobility, did it? And might not all this reverence for ancient authors be a big put-on?

These are fair, indeed essential, hesitations. Let's take the second one first, because we have gone long enough without raising the question of whether reading makes you a better person. The short answer to that question is No. It doesn't. And the long answer doesn't differ too dramatically from the short one.

Now, it's not clear that Machiavelli *wholly* deserves his reputation for scheming, double-dealing, and outright treachery, but if he doesn't, there are plenty of other devoted readers who deserve even worse. Responding to the claim that not just reading but "high culture" in general is morally improving, Terry Eagleton points out that, during World War II, "many people were indeed deep in high culture, but . . . this had not prevented some of them from engaging in such activities as superintending the murder of Jews in central Europe." If reading really was supposed to "make you a better person," then "when the Allied troops moved into the concentration camps . . . to arrest commandants who had whiled away their leisure hours with a volume of Goethe, it appeared that someone had some explaining to do."

So nothing about reading, or listening to Mozart sonatas, or viewing paintings by Raphael necessarily transforms or even improves someone's character. As the eighteenth-century scientist G. C. Lichtenberg once wrote, "A book is like a mirror: if an ass looks in, you can't expect an apostle to look out." Nevertheless, I am going to argue, from time to time throughout the course of this book, that if you really want to become a better person, there are ways in which reading can help. But the degree to which that happens will depend not just on what you read—you have already seen that I am not dictatorial about that—but also why and how. So consider yourself either warned or promised, according to your feelings about moralistic exhortation.

Let us return, then, to Machiavelli in his study. One of the most noteworthy facts about his way of reading his intellectual masters is that it's not passive—reverent, yes, but not passive. "I am not ashamed," he writes, "to speak with them and to ask them the reason for their actions." He is *not ashamed*. He doesn't feel somehow unworthy or unqualified to address them, and indeed to put them to the question, to call them to account for themselves and their ideas. Moreover, for all their greatness his *auctors* take no offense at his boldness: "they in their humanity reply to me."

Now, had Machiavelli met any of those authors in real life, they might not have been so gracious. (It's likely that some of them would be angry about the uses to which Machiavelli put their words.) But one of the wonderful things about books is that they don't grow agitated or dismissive. They patiently bear all the scrutiny you choose to give them, and the more carefully you read them the more of their secrets they yield. It's as though they are *asking* to be put to the question, announcing their readiness to be investigated.

Moreover, it seems clear that to publish a book is to invite a response. True, authors' characters are variable, and some of them are tolerant only of certain responses. George Eliot was so wounded by bad reviews that her lover and companion George Henry Lewes used to go through the papers and magazines to make sure she never saw one. And Brendan Gill tells a story about the American writer John O'Hara, who, among his many accomplishments, wrote the book for the Broadway musical *Pal Joey*: when some friends passed him on the streets of New York and told him that they had just seen *Pal Joey* again and had enjoyed it even more than they had the first time, O'Hara snapped, "What was wrong with it the first time?"

Still, writerly sensitivity aside, those who want no response at all are unlikely to publish a book; and a good many writers are mature enough to know that they have to take the bad with the good. We publish at least in part because we want a personal connection. The more positive that connection the better, of course, but it must be human. And that means that, ideally, there will be something independently thoughtful and constructive in the reader's response. "I agree with every word you write" would be a gratifying thing to hear, I imagine—I wouldn't know—but even more gratifying would be a reader who carries your idea a step further, who adds thoughts you never had that enrich your understanding of your own project. Even the reader who is critical in a genuinely constructive spirit is better, I think, than the reader who, however appreciative, is wholly passive. I can't help but think that Machiavelli's favorite writers would have deeply appreciated his questions, pointed though those inquiries sometimes must have been.

The Russian polymath Mikhail Bakhtin—one of the titanic minds of the twentieth century, though too neglected now—believed that in a dialogue the position of primacy is with the person who listens rather than the one who first speaks. After all, he said, we do not speak unless we anticipate a response; and we shape what we say in light of possible reactions. If the listener—even if only an imagined listener, or our own image of our Self—were not there, we might not speak at all, and if we did we would speak very differently than in fact we do. In Bakhtin's account, this situation means that listeners and readers owe a response to speakers and writers. Passivity is not enough, even if it's very attentive. Reading is more challenging and more enjoyable—more worth the candle—if we are willing to answer the questions a text puts to us, even (or especially) if those questions are implicit. So Alberto Manguel: "The existence of the text is a silent existence, silent until the moment in which a reader reads it. Only when the able eye makes contact with the markings on the tablet does the text come to active life. All writing depends on the generosity of the reader."

The alternative is nicely summed up in a brief sketch Anthony Trollope makes of a minor character in his novel *The Prime Minister*: "He had read much," Trollope says of Everett Wharton, "and though he generally forgot what he read, there were left with him from his readings certain nebulous lights, begotten by other men's thinking, which enabled him to talk on most subjects." I suppose being able to talk on most subjects is something, but not really all we might want from reading. And Trollope refrains from saying that Everett could talk *intelligently*. Wharton reads enough to stock his mind with a few goods, but he never imagines trading those goods in the intellectual marketplace.

Now, when we read something complex or in another way difficult, we may not know what to think about it. But that's when, like Machiavelli, we ask questions. Of course, if you speak a question into the pages of a book there's not much point in holding it up to your ear for an answer. The technology doesn't work like that, as the one-time slave Olaudah Equiano (ca. 1745–1797) discovered: "I had often seen my master and [my friend] Dick employed in reading; and I had a great curiosity to talk to the books, as I thought they did; and so to learn how all things had a beginning: for that purpose I have often taken up a book, and have talked to it, and then put my ears to it, when alone, in hopes it would answer me; and I have been very much concerned when I found it remained silent."*

But if you write the question in the book's margin—even if you just scrawl a question mark—you are marking the scene of your confusion. You are registering your puzzlement, not for the book's sake but for your own sake. The interruption in the flow of your reading is a significant event, and you are quite literally taking note of it. Writing out the whole of your question is better than just flinging a question mark onto the page, because doing the former takes more time—it gets you out of the flow of mere passive reception—and because it forces you to articulate the precise nature of your vexation. A mere question mark could indicate

---

*Thus also, from the other end of the history of literacy, one might say, this brilliant story from *The Onion*, "Nation Shudders at Large Block of Uninterrupted Text" (March 9, 2010):

WASHINGTON—Unable to rest their eyes on a colorful photograph or boldface heading that could be easily skimmed and forgotten about, Americans collectively recoiled Monday when confronted with a solid block of uninterrupted text.

Dumbfounded citizens from Maine to California gazed helplessly at the frightening chunk of print, unsure of what to do next. Without an illustration, chart, or embedded YouTube video to ease them in, millions were frozen in place, terrified by the sight of one long, unbroken string of English words.

"Why won't it just tell me what it's about?" said Boston resident Charlyne Thomson, who was bombarded with the overwhelming mass of black text late Monday afternoon. "There are no bullet points, no highlighted parts. I've looked everywhere—there's nothing here but words."

confusion, disagreement, a feeling of lacking information—any
one of a dozen things. When you write out your question you
render the discomfort exactly.

This is important for two reasons. First, it sharpens your
readerly attention now. Having formulated what's bothering
you, you have it clearly in your mind, and so when you return to
the text you will be readier to note anything that answers your
question or eliminates your confusion. Second, it's a mnemonic
device: the written-out question allows you at some later point
to recapture what you were experiencing when you first read a
passage—something that's intrinsically interesting but also often
quite useful.

For the poet Charles Simic such responses are utterly necessary:

> Wherever and whatever I read, I have to have a pencil, not
> a pen—preferably a stub of a pencil so I can get close to the
> words, underline well-turned sentences, brilliant or stupid ideas,
> interesting words and bits of information, and write short or
> elaborate comments in the margins, put question marks, check
> marks and other private notations next to paragraphs that only
> I—and sometimes not even I—can later decipher. I would love
> to see an anthology of comments and underlined passages by
> readers of history books in public libraries, who despite the strict
> prohibition of such activity could not help themselves and had
> to register their complaints about the author of the book or the
> direction in which humanity has been heading for the last few
> thousand years.

I admire this passage for several reasons, among them Simic's
ability to take delight in something that has always annoyed me:
annotations in library books. He convinces me that I should have
more generosity of spirit, that my support of engaged reading

should exceed my dislike at being distracted by readers who got to a book before I did.

(And at this point I should acknowledge another important and troubling truth: that those who write in library books may do so because they are admirably irrepressible and responsive readers *who can't afford their own books*. Even when they write in library books and thereby make the most of their reading experience, they have to return the books and may not be able to revisit their notes later. The reading of borrowed books can be powerful, but suffers from distinct limitations. Almost everything I have written in these pages assumes something that in the history of reading has rarely been true: abundant and inexpensive books. I have to make an effort to remember what an extraordinary blessing this is.[*])

The case Simic makes for annotation is vivid and strong, but his absolutism suggests that you can overdo this kind of thing. The more heavily you annotate a text—the more questions you ask and comments you venture—the more often you disrupt the continuity of reading. There are times when I have thought that a book or article was choppy and disorganized,

---

[*] Charles Lamb, in his sweet essay "Detached Thoughts on Books and Reading" (1822), writes, "There is a class of street-readers, whom I can never contemplate without affection—the poor gentry, who, not having wherewithal to buy or hire a book, filch a little learning at the open stalls—the owner, with his hard eye, casting envious looks at them all the while, and thinking when they will have done. Venturing tenderly, page after page, expecting every moment when he shall interpose his interdict, and yet unable to deny themselves the gratification, they 'snatch a fearful joy.' Martin B——, in this way, by daily fragments, got through two volumes of *Clarissa* [one of the longest novels in the English language], when the stallkeeper damped his laudable ambition, by asking him (it was in his younger days) whether he meant to purchase the work. M. declares, that under no circumstances of his life did he ever peruse a book with half the satisfaction which he took in those uneasy snatches."

when (I later realized) the real problem was that I had been so active in my commentary that I had disabled myself from following a flow that was actually there. I was blaming the road for my own riding of the brakes. There's a balance to be kept here, and it varies from one reading experience to another. Some books require a lot of commentary, others only a little; and then there are those that we really shouldn't read with pencil in hand at all. Lord help the person who annotates a Harry Potter book or the latest John Grisham. In books of that kind momentum is not to be squandered.*

Not everyone would agree. "Reading is useless, vain, and silly when no writing is involved, unless you are reading Thomas a Kempis or some such. Although I would not want even that kind of reading to be devoid of all note-taking." That's the seventeenth-century Jesuit Jeremias Drexel, and his sneer at

---

*But again, social and personal contexts matter. In an interview about his fascinating memoir *Losing My Cool: How a Father's Love and 15,000 Books Beat Hip-hop Culture*, Thomas Chatterton Williams discussed the differences between his father's way of reading and his own: "Pappy is in his 70s and to this day he still underlines articles in the newspaper every morning. My father loves to read, but he can't simply relax with a good book. Reading will always be work for him. He always felt pressure to read for the purpose of obtaining practical knowledge (even from novels). He was born black in the segregated south in the 1930s, and he figured out early on that if he didn't teach himself what he needed to know through books no one else would. I contrast this with my own view that it's nice to enjoy literature for purely aesthetic reasons.

"In college and in my early 20s, I read for the latter reason mainly, for beauty and quixotic epiphany, both of which are valuable things, but a bit luxurious, too. Today, as a writer and someone who cares deeply about sentences, I find myself reading for many more practical reasons than I used to. I read for technical and inspirational knowledge about my craft. In that way I am more like my father than I used to be. However, I'm also always on the lookout for beauty for beauty's sake and nothing more. I see it both ways now."

reading-without-writing is even more forceful in the original Latin: such reading is *Otiosa, vana, nugatoria*. (It's noteworthy that Drexel seems to think of *The Imitation of Christ* as light reading, perhaps the early modern equivalent of *Chicken Soup for the Soul*.) But if you were determined to take notes on *The Stand* or *Twilight*, what in the world would you write? It's only when you read challenging and complex books without that pencil that you are forgoing an opportunity for meaningful and substantive interaction—and for recording that interaction so your future self can benefit from it.

"Scholars have always made notes," says the English historian Keith Thomas.

> It was common for Renaissance readers to mark key passages by underlining them or drawing lines and pointing fingers in the margin—the early modern equivalent of the yellow highlighter. According to the Jacobean educational writer John Brinsley, "the choycest books of most great learned men, and the notablest students" were marked through, "with little lines under or above" or "by some prickes, or whatsoever letter or mark may best help to call the knowledge of the thing to remembrance." [Isaac] Newton used to turn down the corners of the pages of his books so that they pointed to the exact passage he wished to recall. J. H. Plumb once showed me a set of Swift's works given him by G. M. Trevelyan; it had originally belonged to Macaulay, who had drawn a line all the way down the margin of every page as he read it, no doubt committing the whole to memory. The pencilled dots in the margin of many books in the Codrington Library at All Souls are certain evidence that A. L. Rowse was there before you.

"Pencilled dots"—like some idiosyncratic personal Braille?—surely must be the least intrusive form of marginal commentary.

Rouse must have been a courteous man as well as a careful reader. But Thomas goes on to point out that in early modern times scholars employed "a more brutal method": "to cut the pages out of the book and incorporate them in one's notes. More than one Renaissance scholar cut and pasted in this way, sometimes even from manuscripts. It enabled them to accumulate material which it would have taken months to transcribe." (I have been thankful, in the writing of my recent books, to have recourse to the digital version of this practice, which allows metaphorical *pasting* without literal *cutting*—how admirably nondestructive.)

Those of us who were trained as scholars may tend to over-annotate, but I think it's fair to say that most other readers suffer the opposite temptation. Reading with a writing instrument in hand is an unnatural act for many readers, yet I think in most cases it is necessary to attentive response. You may be able to tell from what I've said so far that I am not a fan of the highlighter. Highlighters allow you very quickly and easily to mark a text, but only by covering it with a bright color; and the very quickness and easiness of the process are inimical to the kind of responsiveness I'm recommending. (There's something to Simic's preference for the stub of a pencil and the intimacy with the page it enforces.) With a highlighter you can have a text marked before you've even had time to ask yourself why you're marking it; and while you might be able to add a question mark or exclamation point in the margin, that will be the limit of your inter-action. And such marks are often quite hard to see after they dry.

I tend to use a mechanical pencil myself, because its line is precise and sharp enough that my marginal annotations are legible, but thick enough to make underlining reliably linear. When I try underlining with a fine-point pen I invariably produce lines that look like paths meandering through a forest—and then of course I can't erase the damned things. But perhaps your manual dexter-ity is such that you need not fear such events. You just need to employ an instrument that allows you to write a few words in the margins—words that you can read later on.

Some books don't make this easy because their margins are too narrow. I don't worry about the margins while reading a science-fiction or fantasy novel for fun, because I won't have a pencil in my hand anyway; and on the off-chance that I do come across something I want to note, I can just dog-ear the page. (A student was in my office recently with her copy of a novel we are reading in class, and I noticed that she had dog-eared maybe seventy or eighty pages in a four-hundred page book. This was commendable in one sense, but how in the world could she ever remember why she had dog-eared any particular page?) But when the words of an ambitious and learned book, a book that demands my most atten-tive strategies of reading, are crammed into pages with the merest ribbon of white space around the edges, I have a problem.

But I am nothing if not resourceful, so I have a system by which I can indicate the need for an annotation and then make that anno-tation at the back of the book, where—thanks to the arithmetic of printing, which requires the number of pages in a book to be divisible by sixteen—there are usually a few blank pages ripe for filling with my queries and exclamations. However, when there are no such blank pages, and no room in the margin, I am defeated. (This happened to me when I read the Vintage paperback edition of Jacques Ellul's *The Technological Society*, which has 7-millimeter margins—yes, I measured them—and nowhere to write com-ments at the back of the book. Underlining and the occasional **?** or **✓** were my only options.)

Now, interestingly, this problem is solved, or at least mitigated, by electronic reading devices like Amazon's Kindle or Sony's Reader, each of which allows the reader to make much lengthier annotations than is feasible in the margins of a paper book— though in a way that generates some mixed blessings.

Kindling ☞ This would be an appropriate time to pause and reflect—for the first time but by no means the last—on technologies of reading other than the familiar object made from bound leaves of paper. In general, when I use the term "book" I will be referring to texts long enough to be bound between covers, whether they actually are bound between such covers or not. *Great Expectations* is a book whether you read it on a Kindle or on a Nook or on an iPad or on an iPhone or on your laptop or on loose sheets of paper printed from a Project Gutenberg e-text or on a paper codex or even on a papyrus scroll. In any of those incarnations it remains *Great Expectations*—still in a deeply meaningful sense *the same book*, a point that bears emphasis, given certain common anxieties about the advent of electronic reading. And on those occasions when I need to make distinctions among the various technologies of reading, "codex" is the word I will use to describe that rectangular thing made of paper pages bound on one side to form a "spine."*

With those clarifications in mind, let's return to the matter of note-taking. To this point, in describing that activity I have been

---

*"Codex" is a Latin word meaning "block of wood." In the ancient world the primary medium for the written word was the scroll, but scrolls were not very portable and were easily damaged; moreover, collections of them could be difficult to organize. Gradually there arose an alternative: a pair of small, thin wooden boards between which sheets of papyrus could be placed, the whole apparatus held together by leather strips threaded through holes in the boards and the papyrus. These became quite fashionable among the Romans because they could be carried around and used to take quick notes: the first PDAs. Eventually people came to see that the codex was in most ways preferable to the scroll—in addition to being sturdier and more portable, it was cheaper, because you could write on both sides of a sheet—and scrolls eventually faded from use. Curiously, the early Christians were among the earliest adopters of the codex: in the second hundred years of Christianity almost all surviving Christian documents are codices, while most other groups, including Jews, stuck with the scroll.

silently assuming that you are reading a codex. After all, a pencil is of little use when you're holding a Kindle, which leads us to ask: What is the role of note-taking when you're reading electronically?

This is a difficult question to answer, it turns out, in part because the technologies that make most e-readers work enforce a strict distinction between two kinds of annotative activity. (There are some e-readers that work with a stylus, but as I write these words none of them have made much of an impact in the market.) When you're reading a codex with a pencil in hand, you might scribble a comment in the margin—which could be comprised of words but also symbols: stars, exclamation points, checkmarks—or you might circle a key word, or you might underline a key passage. All this is done with the same technology, employed in the same way. But on most e-readers you use one entry method to underline or highlight text, another one to type in comments, and a third one to "book-mark" the page (that is, virtually dog-ear it). I'm a proud and happy Kindle owner and I have enjoyed making those notes and also being able to browse through all my notes to all my books in one handy location, but there are significant drawbacks to these technologies as well.

For one thing, you have to think not only about what you want to take note of but also about the method most appropriate to not-ing it. For another, if your reading device lacks a stylus, then you can't make any of those familiar non-alphabetic marks, or can't make them in as easy or useful a way. Over my several decades as a reader I have developed an entire symbolic language for annotat-ing, in which an exclamation point means something quite differ-ent from a question mark, a star, or a checkmark (all of which can be combined with underlinings and circlings). Moreover, e-reader annotation separates your comments from what you're responding to. On the Kindle especially getting to your own annotations is a laborious process, and then you have to go back and forth between them and the text that prompted them.* Now, this might well be a feature rather than a bug if you're reading *someone else's* book: what's more annoying than a library book filled with a previous reader's scribbles?—especially if, as is usually the case, the scribbler offers little insight.

(There are, to be sure, other circumstances in which simultaneous viewing of text and someone else's commentary might be useful. The paradigmatic example of this would be the Talmud, indeed all rabbinical commentary on the Hebrew scriptures, where text and comment flow together on the page. Similarly, though on a less exalted plane, two hundred years ago people lent their books to the poet Coleridge just in order to have, upon the books' return, the great man's marginal notations; but Coleridge, alas, like Rashi and Rabbi Akiba, has long been a-moldering in the grave, which means that trying to read books others have marked up is usually a frustrating process.)

How delightful it would be, then, to have others' notes safely stowed away out of sight unless you decide you want to see them. But your own notes—that's a different story. They are an invaluable record of your encounter with another mind; they mark your excitements, your confusions, your moments of surprise or anger or delight. They fix a history of meaningful experience that would otherwise unmoor itself from memory's dock.

Of course, reading experiences recorded on the page can produce embarrassment later on. I have often, over the years,

---

*Amazon has recently made it possible to look at all your notes and highlights for a given book on their Web site, which is interesting and valuable: it's like seeing laid out on a page the history of your response to a book. This also makes it possible to look at those notes on the screen and then at the book itself on either the Kindle or the Kindle application for your PC—which is something, I guess, but extremely unwieldy in comparison to seeing your notes surrounding the text.

cringed to see how excited I once was about passages that seemed profound to a young reader but to my older and supposedly wiser self fall flat; and I have often been tempted to erase marginal comments that I can no longer endorse, especially since I don't even like my long-ago handwriting. But I *don't* erase those comments; it's valuable to me to have a record of how I once read books, and not just so that I can congratulate myself on the levels of maturity I have achieved. I made a point of writing "*supposedly wiser self.*" I do read differently now than I did thirty years ago, and in many cases I am sure that I read better. But surely not in all. When I was twenty, the most important book in the world to me was William Faulkner's novel *Absalom, Absalom!*—a book that I find nearly unreadable now, even though I can still perceive its greatness. My impatience with Faulkner's style may not mark a maturation on my part, but a narrowing of taste, which is something that many people experience as they age. When I pick up my old and yellowed Vintage paperback of Faulkner's masterpiece and see the excited annotations of my young self, I may cringe at times—but I may also feel a bit of envy of a young man who was able to get so much out of that story. And were it not for the annotations I am not sure I would remember, with any vividness, what *Absalom, Absalom!* meant to me.*

---

*There are many ways in which reading can be a social as well as a private activity, and here is one of them: I read *Absalom, Absalom!* for a class in twentieth-century American literature that my then-girlfriend—now my wife of thirty years—was also taking. She came to love the book as much as I did, and one of my strongest memories from that period of my life is of watching her read that book. I had finished it myself, and sat in her parents' living room while she read at the table in the adjoining dining room. It was a warm and windy evening, and the white lace curtains kept billowing through the open window behind her, sometimes brushing against her back. But for an hour, maybe two, she never noticed, never lifted her head from the story on the page.

At this point some may be muttering that this is all well and good, but writing such comments is enormously time-consuming. It slows you down. It allows you to read fewer books. To those complaints I reply, Yes. It is, it does, and it does. And those are good things.

Slowly, slowly ☞ There's a Web site called *bkkeepr* that provides what its maker would call a service. I am inclined to disagree.

Here's how *bkkeepr* works: the site asks you to have a Twitter account and to use Twitter to send messages to *bkkeepr* when you start a book and again when you finish one. (You can also choose to bookmark a page by sending *bkkeepr* a message identifying that page, but I cannot tell why you would want to do that rather than, say, just dog-earing a page or using a Post-It note. Also, I cannot think of any reason why the site can't be called "bookkeeper" or "Bookkeeper.") *bkkeepr* requires you, when you start a book, to identify it not by the title and author but by the ISBN number. It does so because its whole purpose is to show you how *fast* you read, and it therefore needs the ISBNs in order to identify the particular edition of a book that you're reading.

I think this is a bad idea. It's what you're reading that matters, and how you're reading it, not the speed with which you're getting through it. Reading is supposed to be about the encounter with other minds, not an opportunity to return to the endlessly appealing subject of Me. Americans have enough encouragements to narcissism; let's try to do without this one.

Consider in this light the far more dreadful *1001 Books You Must Read Before You Die*. Leaving aside its absolute violation of the sovereignty of Whim—given the length of the list and the brevity of life, if you enslave yourself to this tome's tyranny you'll never read another word just for the hell of it—let's just focus on the salient fact that this book is not about reading at all. *1001 Books You Must Read Before You Die* is the perfect guide for those who don't want to read but who want to *have read*.

As we saw earlier, the young Richard Rodriguez, seeking some kind of confirmation of his intellectual legitimacy, kept his own score, and flogged himself mercilessly through books that meant nothing to him just so he could cross them off his list. But eventually he saw the emptiness and intrinsic frustration of such an endeavor: he wasn't building his interior culture, he was just moving his eyes across ink-marks. To some extent he did so in order to gain the approval of his teachers, and surely it is common to want to have read to gain accreditation in the eyes of others. And not just teachers; there's also the desire to drop casual mentions at parties of the intellectually stimulating and culturally sophisticated reading you've been doing. Now, I could simply wag a finger here and emphasize the importance of developing independence from others' judgments, a mature indifference to their assessments of your (or anyone's) reading habits. And indeed that would be a wise course to follow. But for those who struggle to achieve such moral self-sustenance, there is an alternative. It's called *lying*.

Yes, lying is wrong. But sometimes in this world we have to choose among evils. It is wrong to lie, but it may be still more wrong to read a bunch of books you don't want to read—and by "read" them I mean cast your eyes across most of the lines on most of the pages—in order to impress people whose opinion you shouldn't be deferring to anyhow. So it would be less bad, I think, take a little time to figure out what people will be impressed to hear that you're reading, use Wikipedia to find out just enough about those books to enable you to bluff plausibly when questioned—and then go back home and *read whatever you want to read*.

And read it at your own pace, without pausing even for a second to think about what your rate of words per minute is. You probably read too fast anyway.

Consider a story by one of the great weirdos of American literature, R. A. Lafferty (1914–2002). It's called "Primary Education of the Camiroi," and it concerns a PTA delegation from Dubuque who visit another planet to investigate an alien society's educational methods. After one little boy crashes into a member of the delegation, knocking her down and breaking her glasses, and then immediately grinds new lenses for her and repairs the spectacles—a disconcerting moment for the Iowans— they interview a girl and ask her how fast she reads. She replies that she reads 120 words per minute. One of the Iowans proudly announces that she knows students of the same age in Dubuque who read five hundred words per minute. (As Stanislas Dehaene explains, that's pretty close to our maximum speed.)

> "When I began disciplined reading, I was reading at a rate of four thousand words a minute," the girl said. "They had quite a time correcting me of it. I had to take remedial reading, and my parents were ashamed of me. Now I've learned to read almost slow enough."

Slow enough, that is, to remember verbatim everything she has read. "We on Camiroi are only a little more intelligent than you on Earth," one of the adults says. "We cannot afford to waste time on forgetting or reviewing, or pursuing anything of a shallowness that lends itself to scanning."*

---

*The Camiroi deal with recalcitrant children by placing them in a pit, without food or water, until they learn their lessons. They deal with extreme cases by hanging. Not that I'm making any recommendations.

The care with which Camiroi children are taught to read enables their teachers to employ a detailed and systematic curriculum. Here for example is the course of study for fourth-graders:

History reading, Camiroi and galactic, basic and geological
Decadent comedy
Simple geometry and trigonometry, hand and machine
Track and field
Shaggy people jokes and hirsute logic
Simple obscenity
Simple mysticism
Patterns of falsification
Trapeze work
Intermediate electronics
Human dissection

Soon after this they begin such subjects as "differential religion," "alcoholic appreciation" (First, Second, and Advanced), and "simple pseudo-human assembly." Granted, the Camiroi *are* more intelligent than we are, so it's doubtful that here on Earth we would be able to introduce hirsute logic or patterns of falsification until seventh grade at the earliest; but we should not underestimate what can be accomplished by those who are willing to read more slowly and with greater care.

Why do people want to read faster? Not least because life is short: "So many books, so little time," as the saying goes. We don't want to miss something special, especially if we miss it because we simply run out of years. This is understandable, and when such thoughts pass through my mind I can feel a brief rush of panic. But—to anticipate a point to be treated later—it's rather odd that I tend not to feel that same panic at the thought of not having time to *re*read books I already love, even though I know that such rereading will surely be pleasurable. The possible pleasure of an unread book weighs more heavily on me than the sure pleasure of one I already know. "Heard melodies are sweet, but those unheard / Are sweeter."

There are also special cases in the world of speedy reading. For instance, Geoff Nicholson writes of a summer in his teenage years when he and a friend competed to see who could read the most: "It wasn't a subtle contest: the winner would be the one who devoured more pages." Nicholson tried science-fiction stories, but his friend chose a shrewder course: "While I slogged across the wastelands of imaginary planets, Rob was gliding through the works of P. G. Wodehouse. It was no contest. I started to read Wodehouse, too, but I lost anyway because Rob simply read faster than I did. But we agreed that Wodehouse was hot stuff, and there was so much of it: 100 or so books (depending on how you count), written over 75 years. For some reason we thought this was a very good thing."

The motivating power of competition in reading is lamentably significant. When I was in the sixth grade, my teacher, with an extraordinary lack of discretion, timed the class in reading. We were given a passage to read and given the green flag to start. When we were finished, we were to fling up our hands so Miss Killian could note the time. I knew that I was one of the fastest readers in class but had some fears about the prowess of one Kimberly, a tall and somber Smart Girl. Sure enough, Kimberly beat me by a few seconds—and then, to add to the humiliation, on the comprehension quiz that followed she got 95 percent to my 70. (Come to think of it, maybe Miss Killian knew what she was doing after all, and meant to teach competitive boys like me a lesson about the costs of reckless, speed-obsessed reading.) That I remember these details so vividly after nearly half-a-century perhaps does not speak well of me.

But, all things considered, I believe that most people read quickly because they want not to read but to have read. But why do they want to have read? Because, I think, they conceive of reading simply as a means of uploading information to their brains. Consider this story from Don Tapscott's book *Grown Up Digital*: Tapscott met a young man named Joe O'Shea, then the president of the student government at Florida State University and a just-chosen Rhodes Scholar, and heard him speak to a lunchtime gathering of "the leaders of Florida State University." O'Shea said of reading,

> I don't read books per se. I go to Google and I can absorb relevant information quickly. Some of this comes from books. But sitting down and going through a book from cover to cover doesn't make sense. It's not a good use of my time as I can get all the information I need faster through the web.

And if all reading were simply a matter of hoarding data—what Nicholas Carr calls "strip-mining of 'relevant content' "—Joe O'Shea, obviously a very smart guy, has an excellent strategy. Likewise, if we grant the same point, we'll be excited about the possibility Stanislas Dehaene mentions of finding means to run text across our visual field more quickly, so that genuine speed-reading becomes possible for the first time.

But if you think of reading in this way, as a means of uploading data, then reading will *always* seem too slow. If I can transfer the complete contents of a book to my computer in ten seconds, why does it take me a week to transfer it to my brain? And why is that latter form of uploading so error-prone and so often incomplete? Note that the Camiroi, for all the wonderful elements of their educational system, share this model of reading: they mandate slow reading not because they think slowness is intrinsically good, but because they want to ensure perfectly accurate transference of data. They're following the best practices of information theory: they're building a redundant system.

Now, the uploading model of reading is a generally valid one in many cases. That's how to read a cookbook or a software manual—though even in those we still have to translate what we have uploaded into meaningful and appropriate action. And while I and my fellow teachers might not be happy about it, that's how many students will read literature and philosophy. We would love it if this young woman staring at Marcus Aurelius's *Meditations* were moved to rethink her concept of the Good, or if that young fellow had his whole scale of values altered by his encounter with *To the Lighthouse*, but we would be foolish to *expect* anything of the kind to happen. After all, if we have assigned those books, we are probably testing our students' understanding of them in some way, and therefore by our actions are virtually demanding that students read instrumentally, that is, for some good completely external to the pleasures and values of reading itself: in other words, we are telling them to read for a grade. And any student who has a grade in the forefront, or perhaps even in the background, of his or her mind is likely to read in that uploading style, so the necessary data will be available when it's needed.

(The astonishing thing is that, from time to time, students really do rethink the Good when reading ancient philosophy and allow Virginia Woolf to disrupt their whole scale of values. And, when this kind of thing happens to readers, they will often feel that the book they just read ended too soon, that they read it too quickly.)

In any event, we need not worry here about grades and instrumentality, because we operate under the sign of Whim. We read what we want, when we want, and there is no one to assign or to evaluate. We are free readers. And for us, the attempt to read

noninstrumental texts in an instrumental way—to read fiction
or poetry or history or theology or even what the bookstores call
"current events" as quickly as possible and with the goal of accurate
transference of data—is not a good idea. It is in fact a perfect recipe
for boredom, because, though few people realize it, many books
become more boring the faster you read them.

This really shouldn't be surprising. Especially if a book is artfully
written—if its language is unusually vivid or lovely, or if its presentation of ideas or images is subtle and surprising—its best features may
be easily passed over by the rapid reader. And this is true not just of
fiction or poetry or drama, but of many works of nonfiction as well.
Careful writers of narrative, whether that narrative is fictional or
historical or journalistic, will, like composers, work with themes and
variations on those themes. For example, consider once more our
friend Gibbon: reading his account of Rome's decline and fall a few
years ago, I noticed his fondness for a particular adverb: *insensibly*.
"It was by such institutions that the nations of the empire insensibly
melted away into the Roman name and people." "We have already
seen that the active and successful zeal of the Christians had insensibly diffused them through every province and almost every city of
the empire." "The heart of Theodosius was softened by the tears of
beauty; his affections were insensibly engaged by the graces of youth
and innocence: the art of Justina managed and directed the impulse
of passion; and the celebration of the royal nuptials was the assurance
and signal of the civil war."*

---

* Once I noticed, or thought I noticed, the unusual prevalence of this word, I went
to Project Gutenberg (http:gutenberg.org), that vast repository of public domain texts,
downloaded the complete text of the *Decline and Fall* and ran a simple search for the
words "insensible" and "insensibly." They proved to be even more prominent than I had
expected. Viva digital technology!

Why does Gibbon like this word so much? Is it just a verbal quirk? I think not: rather, it embodies a key theme of the whole history, which is that major transformations in the life of the Roman empire happened slowly, gradually, and without anyone noticing them: people were *insensible* to the changes, and by the time anyone figured out what had happened, it was too late for a reversal of course. And this insensibility affects political structures, social and religious developments, military cultures, and the hearts of emperors alike; this particular theme has many and wide-ranging variations.

The reader who notices this word, then, notices a vital, not a trivial, point about the story Gibbon tells. But the reader in a hurry isn't going to notice it—and, let's face it, it's hard not to be in a hurry when you're reading a book that in small print exceeds two thousand pages and even in an abridged edition pushes a thousand. Picking up the hefty volumes of Gibbon's complete history (usually there are three of them), the reader can't help but ask, "How much of my life am I willing to commit to these things?" It was the Duke of Gloucester who supposedly said, upon seeing a new installment of the great history, "Another damned thick, square book! Always scribble, scribble, scribble, eh, Mr. Gibbon?" But there is surely something of the Duke in all of us.

And, of course, a book the thickness and squareness of Gibbon's is unthinkable for people who struggle to read any book at all. Let's

---

I have also used Project Gutenberg to download many public-domain books that I have then transferred to my e-reader. (In fact, about three-fourths of the books on my e-reader are such freebies.) But I would not recommend that anyone read Gibbon in this way. Gibbon is famous for the number and cleverness of his footnotes, which in all print editions are in the main text, often in the margin rather than at the foot of the page. (This was the practice in Gibbon's day.) No digital version of the *Decline and Fall* can as yet reproduce this essential matter of formatting.

recall here Nicholas Carr's comment, first cited in the introductory section: "Immersing myself in a book or a lengthy article used to be easy. My mind would get caught up in the narrative or the turns of the argument, and I'd spend hours strolling through long stretches of prose. That's rarely the case anymore. Now my concentration often starts to drift after two or three pages. I get fidgety, lose the thread, begin looking for something else to do." Few of us, I imagine, can say that we don't recognize just what Carr is talking about here.

Our patron saint (stretching the term "saint" a bit) could be John Self, the protagonist of Martin Amis's 1984 novel *Money*. Self is not what you'd call a reader. He may be living in the pre-Internet days, but he has access to telephones, and directs television commercials for a living. He's used to thinking in thirty-second bites. However, John Self is also enamored of a woman who won't talk to him until he reads a book she gives him. "Martina's present was called *Animal Farm* and was by George Orwell. Have you read it? Is it my kind of thing?" Perhaps not, since Self runs aground on the first sentence—"Mr. Jones, of the Manor Farm, had locked the henhouses for the night, but was too drunk to remember to shut the pop-holes"—because he doesn't know what pop-holes are. (Neither did I when I read the book, I might add. But I didn't try to find out and I didn't stop reading.)

Still, Martina is alluring, so he doesn't give up. "I positioned the lamp and laid out the cigarettes in a row. I then drank so much coffee that by the time I cracked the book open on my lap I felt like a murderer getting his first squeeze of juice from the electric chair." Fearful of boredom, Self may have overdone the caffeine; he has trouble keeping on track. The animals' meeting, which begins a couple of pages in, doesn't keep his attention very well.

> [Orwell's] book kicked off with the animals holding a meeting and voicing grievances about their lives. Their lives did sound

rough—just work, no hanging out, no money—but then what
did they expect? I don't nurse realistic expectations about
Martina Twain. I nurse unrealistic ones. It's amazing, you know,
what big-earning berks can get these days. If you're heterosexual,
and you happen to have a couple of bob, you can score with the
top chicks. The top prongs are all going gay, or opting for porno-
graphic berk women. At the animals' meeting, they sing a song.
Beasts of England. . . . I went and lay down on the sack. My head
was full of interference.

And things don't get much better for Self from here on. "This
body of mine is a constant distraction. Here I am, trying to read,
busy reading, yet persistently obliged to put the book aside in
order to hit the can, clip my nails, shave, throw up, clean my
teeth. . . ." Note that he is "obliged" to perform these acts by his
rebellious body. "I started reading again. I went on reading for so
long that I became obsessed by how long I had gone on reading.
I called Selina." But he does not call Selina (another girlfriend) to
tell her that he has finished the book. After failing to reach her, he
resumes his task, but:

Reading takes a long time, though, don't you find? It takes such a
long time to get from, say, page twenty-one to page thirty. I mean,
first you've got page twenty-three, then page twenty-five, then
page twenty-*seven*, then page twenty-*nine*, not to mention the
even numbers. Then page thirty. Then you've got page thirty-*one*
and page thirty-*three*—there's no end to it. Luckily *Animal Farm*
isn't that long a novel. But novels . . . they're all long, aren't they.
I mean, they're all so *long*. After a while I thought of ringing down
and having Felix bring me up some beers. I resisted the temptation, but that took a long time too. Then I rang down and had Felix
bring me up some beers. I went on reading.

Given all this, why is John Self a saint? Because *he eventually finishes the book*. And I defy anyone, even the most dedicated reader, to claim that Self's experience isn't uncomfortably familiar. It would be familiar to ancient hermits or Tibetan monks as well, give or take a Martina or Selina.

But would John Self have managed to make his lonely way to the end of *Animal Farm*, even spurred on by thoughts of Martina, had he lived in the age of the Internet? With a laptop and free hotel wi-fi I doubt he would have persevered to the animals' song, some eight or nine pages in. In such an environment, how is it even feasible to recommend slower reading? If we read more slowly, won't that just mean that we get through less text before succumbing to distraction?

I'm afraid that just such a result is immensely likely—unless we do some work to alter our habits. That work can be done, and it's worth doing; but even accidental reformations are possible and immensely valuable, as I learned about a year ago. It's an encouraging tale, I think.

True confessions ☞ I've been a devoted reader almost all my life, and for twenty-five years I've been a teacher of literature, but I am as vulnerable to distractions as anyone this side of John Self. A typical day for me begins with a consultation of my RSS reader: I subscribe to about two hundred feeds, and on any given morning I find about a hundred updates to scan, some of which I load in my browser. A few of those I read in full, many I just look over; some go into a service called Instapaper to read later, while others get bookmarked. I also have a blog, an online commonplace book, and a Twitter account, so a good deal of what I read gets redirected to those destinations. They all get morning attention as well, along with whatever email came in during the night.

That would be enough to occupy any sane person, but that RSS reader repopulates itself throughout the day; the people I follow on Twitter tweet away; email continues to trickle, or on some days to flood, in. I could have all of these information channels keep me informed of their updates, but I have a modicum of common sense and so have disabled notifications, so that if I want to know what's new I have to make a point of checking. I would love to be able to report that I get so absorbed in my work that I never do that, but alas, I rotate through the possibilities for informational novelty often. (I actually do not know how often and prefer not to think about it.) Moreover, I have access to all these sources of stimulation on my iPhone, which I have with me most of the time. In fact, I am very rarely without the option of going online.

The philosopher William James famously wrote of the "blooming, buzzing confusion" that constitutes sensuous experience for babies, who have not yet developed the filters necessary to organize that experience into discrete and meaningful units, but our daily technologies threaten to return us all to virtual babyhood. And over the years this blooming and buzzing has had a significant effect on my own ability to read for any length of time. Like Nicholas Carr, I get twitchy within just a few minutes of sitting down with a book—I have noticed that my hand will start reaching for my iPhone without my consciously telling it to, as though I am becoming a digital-era (but I hope slightly less creepy) Dr. Strangelove. About two years ago, I realized that I was reading fewer books than I had since age ten, and reading them less well— with less attention—and therefore getting less pleasure from the reading.

As my symptoms were getting worse and worse, despite my awareness of them, something interesting happened, and, I am pleased to say, it happened in a bookstore. I was standing in my local Borders with a big pile of books in the crook of my arm.

The haul included Neal Stephenson's then-new novel *Anathem*, another hefty Stephenson novel I hadn't managed to catch up to, and a couple of large works of history, including Diarmaid MacCulloch's *The Reformation*. (You will discern that my attention-deficit syndrome had not affected my readerly ambitions, though this was probably a function of sheer denial.) My arm was starting to ache. I found a seat and looked over my hoard. I wanted them all, but the print was pretty small in a couple of them—an increasingly significant factor as my eyes age in ways that optometric technology can only imperfectly address. Most of them, I noted with some concern, because of their size, would be rather awkward to handle. And then, where was I going to put them? Every time I bring books to my house or office I have to get rid of other books, or store them somewhere, in order to make room for the new arrivals.

Forget this, I said to myself. I'm getting a Kindle. And I did.

On my blog I have written much about the Kindle, and I will not rehash all of that here; I just want to emphasize one major point, and do it by way of disagreement with another Kindle user. In a large and smart essay for the journal *The New Atlantis*, Christine Rosen writes, "Much has been written about the Kindle's various features: wireless service that allows for rapid delivery of e-texts; the ability to search the Web; a service called 'NowNow' that performs real-time searches (using human beings!) to answer questions; a dedicated 'Search Wikipedia' function. These features are remarkable—and remarkably distracting." My response to Rosen's claims is that those last three features would indeed be distracting if they were easy to get to, but they aren't, and they aren't designed to be. The Kindle's access to the Web is tucked several clicks away from any book you might be reading. Rosen says she kept getting distracted by those options and couldn't focus on her book, but I wonder how she managed that. For me, it's just too much trouble to get into any of that stuff—it's much easier to keep reading.

· And that's how the Kindle worked for me when I first got it, and for the most part still works today: it kept me reading. Think how easy it is, and how tempting, when you're reading a novel to look ahead to the end. Maybe you just want to see how many pages there are in the book, to know how much you have left to read—but, of course, you just might sneak a peek at the last paragraph while you're at it. You can do this on the Kindle, but it's difficult. Similarly, when reading many different kinds of book you might want to take a look at the table of contents, to check how many chapters there are, whether they have titles, what the titles might mean, and so on—and again, you can do that on the Kindle, but only by moving your hands in a different and less natural way than you employ to turn the pages as you follow an argument or narrative. (Kindles have clocks, but when you're reading you can't see the time unless you click the Menu button, at which point it appears at the top of the screen. The absence of a clock on the reading screen makes it easier, I think, to escape into the book's own time.)

In short, once you start reading a book on the Kindle—and this is equally true of the other e-readers I've tried—the technology generates an inertia that makes it significantly easier to keep reading than to do anything else. E-readers, unlike many other artifacts of the digital age, promote *linearity*—they create a forward momentum that you can reverse if you wish, but not without some effort. The first book I read onscreen was *Anathem*, a behemoth, and that encounter was delightful because there was no awkward manual management of a large heavy book, and limited temptation to repeatedly investigate the book's apparatus. *Anathem* contains a glossary to help readers deal with Stephenson's many neologisms, but my tendency when offered something like that is to wander around in it and forget to get back to the story. Reading the novel on my Kindle, I knew that I could get to the Glossary if I needed to, but it didn't constantly tempt me. Instead, I became absorbed in the story itself.

I found that when I was seated (or reclining) in a comfortable position, I could hold the Kindle in one hand with my thumb poised over the "Next Page" button, and then do nothing except kick the saccades into gear and click that button. I found my ability to concentrate, and concentrate for long periods of time, restored almost instantly. I am not sure why this happened, though I have some guesses: primarily, I think, an e-reader gives that Strangeloveian hand of mine something to do, and something similar to what it does when it checks email or Twitter on the iPhone. (Muscle memory is my friend.) And I am sure that I benefit from being able to reconnect with the habits of long-term attentiveness that I had built up for decades before going so thoroughly digital. Moreover, when I got an e-reader I immediately read the kind of book it's best suited for, that is, narrative-driven fiction. Had I started with David Hume's *Enquiry Concerning Human Understanding* I might never have persisted with the device.

I don't think that e-readers are going to be a cure-all for everyone in need of cultivating better and longer attention. But I do think that my experience suggests that it's not reasonable to think of "technology"—in the usual vaguely pejorative meaning of that word—as the enemy of reading. The codex is itself a technology, and a supremely sophisticated one, but even digital electronic technologies vary tremendously: e-readers are by any measure *far* less distracting than an iPad or a laptop. It's at least possible for new technologies to be part of the solution instead of part of the problem.

Possible, though perhaps not very likely. Recent digital technologies generate a perfect storm of anti-attention, largely because they draw on the tremendous power of what B. F. Skinner called "intermittent reinforcement." We click the "new mail" button in our email clients or look once more at Twitter or revisit Facebook because we get something new and interesting only *sometimes*—and this, Skinner learned, is far more powerful an incentive to animals than regular and predictable reinforcement. After all, if we *know* that whenever we click the button we will have new mail, our curiosity is diminished: when we get to it, it'll be there. It's the not knowing that prompts my rebellious hand to inch toward the iPhone. As Sam Anderson has written, "The Internet is basically a Skinner box engineered to tap right into our deepest mechanisms of addiction." (Many metaphors for this situation may suggest themselves: I am also fond of Cory Doctorow's comment that "the biggest impediment to concentration is your computer's ecosystem of interruption technologies.")

Many of us try to console ourselves in the midst of the blooming and buzzing by claiming the powers of *multitasking*. But a great deal of very thorough research into multitasking has been done in recent years, and it has produced some unequivocally clear results, chief among them being:

- no one actually multitasks; instead, we shift among different tasks and give attention to only one at any given time;
- the attempt to multitask results in a state of "continuous partial attention";
- those who believe they are skilled multitaskers tend to be worse at it than others.

At the end of this book you'll find references to back up these claims: read 'em and weep. These are facts that every would-be reader has to face, because they are the facts that, above all others, have led so many intelligent and well-educated people to despair of their ability to read books, even when they were once avid book-readers.

This is a situation—and this stage in my argument a moment—which seems to lend itself to *advice*, to *recommendations*. But what would be the point? We all already know what we need to do if we want to get back to reading slowly and attentively. Shut down the computer; put aside the cellphone. If the temptation to check email or texts or Twitter is too strong, then take yourself somewhere where the gadgets aren't. Lock them in the car before you enter the coffee shop with your book; give them to your spouse or partner and request that they be hidden, and then go into a room with a comfortable chair and close the door behind you. It's not hard to come up with handy-dandy practical suggestions; what's hard is *following* them—or rather, even *wanting* to follow them. What's hard is imagining, fully and vividly, the good things that happen when we follow through.*

And we *have* to follow through. More succinctly than I ever could, the late David Foster Wallace explained why, in the commencement address he delivered at Kenyon College in 2005. This address has become famous and widely quoted in the aftermath of Wallace's suicide in 2008, in part because for some people

---

*Nicholas Carr: "The problem today is not that we multitask. We've always multitasked. The problem is that we're always in multitasking mode. The natural busyness of our lives is being amplified by the networked gadgets that constantly send us messages and alerts, bombard us with other bits of important and trivial information, and generally interrupt the train of our thought. The data barrage never lets up. As a result, we devote ever less time to the calmer, more attentive modes of thinking that have always given richness to our intellectual lives and our culture—the modes of thinking that involve concentration, contemplation, reflection, introspection. The less we practice these habits of mind, the more we risk losing them altogether."

Wallace's inability to conquer his own demons yields a certain *frisson* to the earnestness and passion of his advice to graduates. But it's a great address, made all the more moving by our retrospective awareness of just how hard-earned its wisdom was. For our purposes here, this is the key passage:

> Twenty years after my own graduation, I have come gradually to understand that the liberal arts cliché about teaching you how to think is actually shorthand for a much deeper, more serious idea: learning how to think really means learning how to exercise some control over *how* and *what* you think. It means being conscious and aware enough to *choose* what you pay attention to and to choose how you construct meaning from experience. Because if you cannot exercise this kind of choice in adult life, you will be totally hosed.

Lost ☞ The stab of envy came instantly, unexpectedly. I was somewhere quite new to me: on one of the enormous ferries that run between the mainland of British Columbia and Vancouver Island. As we moved westward, we traded shifting clouds for brilliant morning sunshine. My wife and I had every expectation of a delightful day on the island and had even managed to procure some surprisingly good coffee from a helpful machine. We sat at a small round table, sipping the coffee and gazing out at the small islands in the Strait of Georgia; all was well indeed. But then my eye strayed to a neighboring table. There sat a ten-year-old boy, gazing fixedly upon the face of his father, who was reading in an excited whisper from *Harry Potter and the Half-Blood Prince*. It was July 16, 2005. The book had been released just eight hours earlier, at midnight, and it would be days before my own copy landed in my greedy hands.

Though one might say that that boy was being read to rather than reading—a dubious distinction, in my mind—he had something

I wanted. And by that I do not primarily mean that he was finding out Harry's next adventures, but that he was undergoing something powerful and wonderful: he was lost in a book. As Winifred Gallagher has written, "attention enables you to have the kind of Dionysian experience beautifully described by the old-fashioned term 'rapt'—completely absorbed, engrossed, fascinated, perhaps even 'carried away'—that underlies life's deepest pleasures, from the scholar's study to the carpenter's craft to the lover's obsession." The boy was indeed rapt, lost in the story, carried away by the story; the rest of the world, even the morning sun on the sea and the islands dotting the strait, was as nothing to him. And only those who have experienced that complete absorption of the self in something else, something beautiful, know also what it means to have misplaced that capacity; only we know the anxiety that arises from the fear we may never have that again.

This is why attentiveness is worth cultivating: not just because it is good for you or because (as Gallagher also says) it can help you "organize your world," but because such raptness is deeply satisfying. It is, really, what Whim is all about; what Whim is *for*. I even think that such satisfaction is largely what David Foster Wallace has in mind when he says that without attentiveness, and the ability to choose what we attend to, we will be "totally hosed"—because after all, people get by without being able to make such choices. Many of them have very successful lives, in most of the ways that we measure success. But they're missing something, something vital, by never knowing what it's like to be so absorbed.

In his brilliant sequence of poems called "*Horae Canonicae*"* W. H. Auden pictures this blessed condition:

---

*That is, "Canonical Hours," the times traditionally appointed in monasteries for prayer.

You need not see what someone is doing
to know if it is his vocation,

you have only to watch his eyes:
a cook mixing a sauce, a surgeon

making a primary incision,
a clerk completing a bill of lading,

wear the same rapt expression,
forgetting themselves in a function.

How beautiful it is,
that eye-on-the-object look.

For Auden these are the makers of civilization: "There should be monuments, there should be odes, / to the nameless heroes" who first ignored "the appetitive goddesses":

to the first flaker of flints
who forgot his dinner,

the first collector of sea-shells
to remain celibate.

Where should we be but for them?

The "appetitive goddesses" are those—like Aphrodite, goddess of love—who preside over our appetites, our instinctive and inbuilt desires, desires which, by some miracle, we are sometimes able to overcome. The wonderful thing for Auden about that first "flaker of flints" is that he was so absorbed in his work that he *forgot* his dinner: he didn't decide not to have it, he simply failed to notice the growling of his stomach. His eye was utterly fixed on its object.

And there is something even more beautiful, perhaps, when we achieve this "eye-on-the-object look" not because we have found our *vocation* but because we have found our *avocation*—when the reason for our raptness is sheer and unmotivated delight. This is what makes "readers," as opposed to "people who read." To be lost in a book is genuinely addictive: someone who has had it a few times wants it again, and wants it enough, perhaps, to beg a friend to hide the damned BlackBerry for a couple of hours, *please*.

Auden's paleolithic flint-flaker finds a more recent counterpart in the English radical William Cobbett. Cobbett, who was born in 1763, was the son of a laborer and as an adolescent worked as a gardener on a great estate near Richmond. One day, when he had some time off, he decided to visit Kew Gardens, but along the way spotted a copy of Jonathan Swift's *A Tale of a Tub* in the window of a bookseller. "The title was so odd, that my curiosity was excited. I had the [threepence the book cost], but then, I could have no supper." He bought the book and immediately became so caught up in it—even though many of its learned references were inscrutable to him—that he read until it was too dark to see the pages, scarcely noticing his hunger pangs. Later he would ascribe to that moment "a birth of intellect": in Swift's satire he found a model of social conscience, of anger at cruelty, and he discerned also the power of words to channel and embody that anger. The lure of the book so compelled him that he voluntarily gave up a meal in exchange for the chance to read it; and the spell of the book, as he read it, was so strong that neither hunger nor darkness could touch him. He was "rapt"; anyone passing him would have recognized that "eye-on-the-object look."*

---

*A similar story, one that consciously echoes David Copperfield's experience of "reading for life," comes from Robert Collyer (born in 1823), who as a child worked in a linen factory in Fewston, North Yorkshire. Later in life, as a well-known Unitarian minister writing his autobiography, he placed great emphasis on his first purchase of a

In her memoir *Ruined by Reading*, Lynne Sharon Schwartz comments that when she first became a reader, "I thought reading would transform my life, or at least teach me how to live it. It does teach something, many things, but not what I naïvely expected. . . . If no girl was ever ruined by a book, none was ever saved by one either." This may be giving up too much ground. Cobbett's life was really and truly transformed by Swift's book; and in the third circle of Hell Dante meets a woman named Francesca who claims that her life, and that of her lover, was destroyed by a book.*

But in any event, Schwartz is absolutely right to say that "what reading teaches, first and foremost, is how to sit still for long periods and confront time head-on. The dynamism is all inside, an exalted, spiritual exercise so utterly engaging that we forget time and mortality along with all of life's lesser woes, and simply bask in the everlasting present." Few lessons could be more valuable, or more consequential, because to read in this utterly absorbed way I have been describing is to collaborate with a book on the conquest of time. The book you read—or whatever you read—becomes your ally and your chief support as you take ownership of your inner space and banish those forces that would rule your consciousness. Wallace again: "learning how to think really means learning how to

---

book, a child's history of Dick Whittington and his cat: "I have a library now of about three thousand volumes . . . but in that first purchase lay the spark of a fire which has not yet gone down to white ashes, the passion which grew with my growth to read all the books in the early years I could lay my hands on. . . . I see myself in the far-away time and cottage reading, as I may truly say in my case, for dear life." This is one of many wonderful stories related by Jonathan Rose in his great book *The Intellectual Life of the British Working Classes*.

*Though she was married to another man, she and Paolo were so captivated by a love story that they imitated it—as, in a way, did Anna Karenina, as I have already noted. But, of course, those stories would have had no such effect on most others. One must be ready for what a book has to offer in order to experience the most powerful consequences of reading, though it's not always good to be ready.

exercise some control over *how* and *what* you think. It means being conscious and aware enough to *choose* what you pay attention to and to choose how you construct meaning from experience." Replace "think" with "read" and the point is clear.

This is, I suppose, the place where I should insert a rant against all the technologies that attempt to govern time for us, to tell us not only what to do but when to do it: the insistent ring of the phone, the quieter but (for many of us) more frequent chime of an incoming text, a new set of tweets, more email, a refreshed RSS reader . . . and I can do that. But really, the cultivation of attentiveness has *always* been hard for human beings: as long as we have had readers we have had readers frustrated by their inability to concentrate. It is the nature of the human beast.

Abbot Hugh's advice   ☞ There have been, from time to time over the centuries, communities committed to the practice of reading—usually as a distinctively *spiritual* practice, though what they have learned and taught is applicable to readers with nonspiritual needs, if there are any such people. Consider, for instance, the great monastery of St. Victor in Paris in the twelfth century, and its abbot, Hugh, who wrote a treatise for readers called the *Didascalicon*. The title means something like "manual of instruction," and Hugh's book is also, more or less, a theory of education, a brief encyclopedia, and a system for organizing all knowledge. Hugh is primarily interested in creating a system of reading for his fellow monks, but what he has to say is remarkably valuable for people whose motives for reading—and whose decisions about what to read—are far from monastic.*

---

*Hugh would be utterly appalled at the use to which I am putting his ideas, not because the readers of this book are not necessarily monks, but because they are not

I hesitate to invoke Hugh in this book, because few people could be less sympathetic to the rule of Whim than he. First of all, if you have the ability to read but fail to do so because you are "caught up in the affairs and cares of this world more than is needful" or because you are "given over to the vices and sensual indulgences of the body," then Hugh wants you to know that people of your ilk are *valde detestabiles*—"utterly detestable." Moreover, the strictness of his instructional plan makes Adler and Van Doren look like devil-may-care hedonists. But his general model of reading is conceptually brilliant and well worth getting to know—especially for those of us who, like most twelfth-century monks, struggle to keep our attention from flagging.

Hugh begins, attractively enough, by rejecting intellectual snobbery: "I myself never looked down on anything that had to do with education, but . . . often learned many things that seemed to others to be a sort of joke or just nonsense." He commends this attitude to other readers, chiefly because people who begin by occupying their minds with small and trivial things can use what they know as a foundation, or a stepping stone, that allows them to ascend to higher things. The person just beginning to bring some discipline to his or her life as a reader need not be ashamed at reading non-masterpieces, or at only being able to focus on reading a few pages at a time. Let that person, then, begin with short stories or essays and work toward longer works that demand extensive attention. Indeed, it's vital as a reader to move forward in

---

necessarily Christians. For Hugh the purpose of reading is to gain *sapientia* (wisdom), and for him *sapientia* is found in Jesus Christ and not elsewhere. In other respects too I am simplifying and altering Hugh's system, leaving out much that he would think absolutely essential, perhaps especially memory training: Hugh was a great believer in the necessity of developing one's faculties of memorization.

an orderly way (*ordinate procedere debet*): "the man who moves along step by step is the man who moves along best, not like some who fall head over heels when they wish to make a great leap ahead."

Furthermore, Hugh says, the reader who makes progress in these matters should beware of the dangers of pride—the source of intellectual snobbery—because pride can cause you to look down on other readers and simultaneously prevent you from striving toward greater skill and knowledge. Hugh, though he doesn't use this particular terminology in the *Didascalicon*, shared the common medieval belief that human life is a pilgrimage, and each human person is a *viator*, a wayfarer: wayfarers know where they are going, and remain in motion, but also know that they haven't *arrived*.* There is therefore no cause for arrogance toward others who walk the same path: we're all moving "step by step," in an orderly way. On these grounds Hugh particularly insists that the student of reading cultivate the virtue of humility: "For the reader there are three lessons taught by humility that are particularly important: First, that he hold no knowledge or writing whatsoever in contempt. Second, that he not blush to learn from any man. Third, that when he has attained learning himself, he not look down upon anyone else." Armed with this humility, the reader can

---

* In a lovely book called *On Hope*, Josef Pieper explores Thomas Aquinas's theology of hope along these lines: the hopeful person is by definition a wayfarer (*viator*), because the virtue of hope lies midway between the two vices of despair (*desperatio*) and presumption (*praesumptio*). What despairing persons and presumptuous persons have in common is that they aren't going anywhere, they are fixed in place: the despairing because they don't think there's anywhere to go, the presumptuous because they think they have reached the pinnacle of achievement. These distinctions map precisely onto the world of reading. I have addressed this book largely to the despairing, that is, those who believe or fear that serious reading is beyond their reach, but there are lessons here for the overly confident as well.

safely pursue the wisdom to be gained from reading; the reader can become a true *student*.

Ivan Illich—whose account of Hugh I am drawing on heavily here—comments that when he was trying to understand what Hugh meant by *studio* (study), he happened to check not just a Latin dictionary but also the OED, and was pleased and intrigued to find this:

1. (Chiefly in translations from Latin): Affection, friendliness, devotion to another's welfare; partisan sympathy; desire, inclination; pleasure or interest felt in something—NB: All these meanings are obsolete since 1697.

So the *student* of something is (or potentially was, before 1697) not just attentive to what he or she studies, but positively disposed toward it: friendly, even affectionate. The student values the well-being of what he or she studies, wishes for it to flourish. The reader attends to the work itself and the valuable contents therein.

Those valuable contents can only be retrieved, however, by the patient and careful reader. Such a reader must certainly practice *cogitatio*, must cogitate on the text, that is, intellectually discern its meaning as best he or she can. But this is not enough, because, to return to a point we emphasized earlier, such reading is purely reconstructive and therefore nonresponsive. The genuine student will move on from *cogitatio* to *meditatio*, meditation, which for Hugh means "incorporating" the text—if the text is truly worthy, which the serious reader will discern—into the reader's own experience. Randall Jarrell, we may recall, says that the book we read at Whim says to us, "You must change your life": David Copperfield likewise was reading not just for entertainment but "for life" itself. He was being changed, enriched and strengthened and consoled, by what he read.

Let me risk one more Latin word here: for Hugh this meditation, especially on sacred texts, could best be achieved by *ruminatio*, a word which may call to mind something rather more highfalutin' than Hugh intended. For us to "ruminate" is to engage in a pretty dignified, or dignified-sounding, act, but Hugh was thinking of cows and goats and sheep, *ruminant* animals, those who chew the cud. A ruminant beast has multiple stomachs, the first of which, the rumen, can be used for temporary storage: the animal chews some food and swallows it, sending it to the rumen, but then regurgitates the partially digested lump and chews on it some more. Only after rumination does the food get passed to the next stomach, from which there is no return. Hugh believes this is the perfect model of attentive reading: to read the text, to pass it along to the depths of the mind—but then to call it back for further thought. (Hugh's model of reading is notably and consistently *physical*: he wants to train our bodies to be our assistants in reading, surely because he knows what John Self learned, that bodies have a natural propensity to interfere with still and quiet attentiveness. To "incorporate" is literally to take into the body.) If you have ever read a passage and only later realized that you may not have understood it, and have therefore returned to reread it, you are a ruminant reader.

However, as we have seen, powerful cultural and psychological forces inhibit any ruminant instincts we might have. If we are easily distracted, or in a hurry, or if we are wanting to get a book read so we can cross it off our list and move on to the conveyor belt's next item, we may forget about that passage and never regurgitate it for further attention. And this is not just *our* problem: that Hugh goes to such pains to instruct monks in these matters tells us that they had to deal with many of the same temptations we do.

I would encourage those who suffer from such temptations to consider the virtues of poetry—yes, *poetry*. I have taught literature for quite a while now, so I am used to people telling me that while they appreciate and enjoy many novels, they just don't get poems.* But such people are setting up unnecessary barriers for themselves. Poetry, lyric poetry anyway, is perhaps the ideal literary form for our time, as long as we rid ourselves of the notion that poems can be made sense of in a single reading. As I noted earlier, many narratives expect to be read in this way—to be navigated one good time—but it is a mistake to transfer such a model of reading to poems. I often remind my students when I assign them a group of poems to read for a particular class period that I expect them to read each poem slowly, carefully, aloud if possible, and at least five times. I also require students to memorize fifty lines of poetry and recite them to me, for, as George Steiner has often commented, to memorize something is in the truest sense to learn it "by heart." And I have often noticed that when people write papers about poems they have memorized they tend to have a deeper understanding than is usual;

---

*Though this dislike of poetry can be overstressed, as Charles Simic has noted in a reflection on his tenure as Poet Laureate of the United States: "In a country in which schools seem to teach less literature every year, where fewer people read books and ignorance reigns supreme regarding most issues, poetry is read and written more than ever. Anyone who doesn't believe me ought to take a peek at what's available on the web. Who are these people who seem determined to copy almost every poem ever written in the language? Where do they find the time to do it? No wonder we have such a large divorce rate in this country. I won't even describe the thousands of blogs, the on-line poetry magazines, both serious ones and the ones where anyone can post a poem their eight-year[-old] daughter wrote about the death of her goldfish. People who kept after me with their constant emails and letters were part of that world. They wanted me to announce what I propose to do to make poetry even more popular in the United States. Unlike my predecessors who had a lot of clever ideas, like having a poetry anthology next to the Gideon Bible in every motel room in America (Joseph Brodsky), or urging daily newspapers to print poems (Robert Pinsky), I felt things were just fine. As far as I could see, there was more poetry being read and written than at any time in our history."

they seem to have intuited the underlying logic of the poems—they *get* them, even when the poems are quite challenging.

But for most readers, and all nonreaders, poetry intimidates. W. S. Merwin wrote a poem called "Why Some People Do Not Read Poetry," and it begins thus:

> Because they already know that it means
> stopping and without stopping they know that
> beyond stopping it will mean listening

Yes: poems require *stopping*. But then so do many experiences of great value. Stop walking, stop talking, stop browsing the Internet, and *then* kiss your beloved.

And here is the encouraging thing about poetry: a lyric poem requires of you short periods of concentration—shorter by far than, say, *Animal Farm*. You can read it through without losing your focus, as long as you remember that you are not expected to make that reading a comprehensive one. You can then come back to it later, as many times as you wish—and indeed, the more often you come back to it the more greatly it will reward you, if it's really good. Some of the best poems in the world are shorter than the average blog post; and consider this anonymous masterpiece, probably from the sixteenth century:

> O western wind, when wilt thou blow
> That the small rain down can rain?
> Christ, that my love were in my arms
> And I in my bed again!

That's one hundred and thirty characters—you could tweet it. And should. For those who want to appropriate Abbot Hugh's teachings, poetry is perhaps the ideal place to begin.

Let us sum those teachings. For the reader who wishes to follow Whim rather than whim—who has learned enough about what he or she *really* thrives on to seek more of it—the first lessons must be in humility. If you haven't read a novel in the past five years, it might not be best to start with *Anna Karenina* or *Gravity's Rainbow*: don't scruple to enjoy and learn from less challenging works, or poems that for all their challenges are brief: All in the proper *ordo*. (Pause to imagine John Self reading *Ulysses*.) Don't waste time and mental energy in comparing yourself to others, whether to your shame *or* gratification, since we are all wayfarers. Come to what you read with a charitable disposition: don't expect to fight with the text, but instead seek to treat it well; be willing to meet it more than halfway, as though it were a guest in your home, which in a way it is. (In some rare cases you might think of the book as the host, yourself as the guest: Machiavelli's habitual posture suggests that he thought of entering his own library as though he were entering a great king's court.) Above all, take time to discern what this book—or story, or poem, or essay, or article—has to offer you. Slow down. Make a point of revisiting passages that seem especially rich, or especially confusing, or for that matter especially offensive. Chew the textual cud for a while before sending it to the further stomachs of your mind: you may well spare yourself a case of heartburn later.

All this advice may have been meant for Parisian monks eight hundred years ago, but readers today could do a lot worse than follow the practices of the wise and saintly Abbot Hugh.

The triumphant return of Adler and Van Doren ☞ But at this point I have to acknowledge a certain tension: the strategies of reading that Hugh recommends don't fit very well with the kind of "rapt" reading I have celebrated elsewhere. Or so it would seem.

Just as I have discouraged the reading of Stephen King or
J. K. Rowling with annotative pen in hand, I must also admit that
it seems perverse to pause in the midst of such exciting tales for
rumination. All books want our attention, but not all of them want
the same *kind* of attention, and good readers know this and make the
necessary adjustments.

One could parse this situation in a variety of ways. In the
strictest sense, the kind of attention a lyric poem asks is different from that a narrative poem asks, which in turn may
be (slightly or significantly) different from what a novel asks.
How closely related are works of history to novels, then, since
both are long-form narratives? And do academic monographs
differ from popular histories in this respect? And what about
philosophical treatises, textbooks in abnormal psychology,
exercises in Buddhist spirituality . . . ? These may be rabbit trails
from which there is no return. What distinctions will serve us
well here?

Actually, we could do worse than employ the threefold model
of our old friends Adler and Van Doren: reading for *information*,
reading for *understanding*, reading for *entertainment*. These categories aren't perfect—they overlap a good deal—but having spoken
so ill of these authors earlier, I feel that I owe them something
now. So with the caveat that these describe predominant purposes
(or just moods), not absolutely different strategies, I think we can
make use of this tripartite scheme—with the necessary substitu-
tion of *pleasure* for *entertainment*.

When we read for pleasure we don't, or shouldn't, take notes:
being rapt is then our only ambition. When we read for information—the paradigmatic case being the textbook on the contents of
which we are about to be tested—we had *better* take notes. When
we are reading for understanding, we may or may not take notes,
depending on the context. Sometimes we wish to be rapt or are

caught up in the book regardless of whether we wish to be or not; other times we will strive for a more detached analytical mode. (More about this soon.) These can be dramatically different experiences. Do the strategies and practices of the one kind of reading differ so greatly from the other that what we do in the one kind of reading has no bearing on the others? Or, worse, could it be that the one kind of attentiveness is actually inimical to the others, so that the more we read in the one way the less we will be able to read in the second and third?

(One enemy of good reading is confusion about which mode of attention is appropriate to a given book. I am certain that this very confusion makes it almost impossible for anyone to read—genuinely to *read*—the Bible. In both the Hebrew and Christian Bibles, narrative and other more-or-less literary forms are dominant, which seems to call for a strategy of reading for *understanding* similar to what one might use in an encounter with, say, Homer; but these books' status as sacred text suggests, to many modern readers anyway, that their purpose is to provide *information* about God and God's relation to human beings. "Strip-mining" the Psalms, or the Song of Solomon, or even the more elevated discourses of the Gospel of John, "for relevant content" might not seem like a promising strategy, but many generations of pastors have pushed it pretty hard, as though the Bible were no more than an awkwardly coded advice manual.)

I think we must admit that some readers do indeed reach this point of irreconcilable differences among the possible modes of reading. It seems to have happened to Charles Darwin, who wrote in his autobiography, "Up to the age of thirty, or beyond it, poetry of many kinds, such as the works of Milton, Gray, Byron, Wordsworth, Coleridge, and Shelley, gave me great pleasure, and even as a schoolboy I took intense delight in Shakespeare, especially in the historical plays. . . . But now for many years I cannot endure to read a line of poetry: I have tried lately to read Shakespeare, and found it so intolerably dull that it nauseated me. I have also almost lost my taste for pictures or music."

Darwin found this alteration in his mind deeply worrisome:

> My mind seems to have become a kind of machine for grinding
> general laws out of large collections of facts, but why this should
> have caused the atrophy of that part of the brain alone, on which
> the higher tastes depend, I cannot conceive. A man with a mind
> more highly organised or better constituted than mine, would
> not, I suppose, have thus suffered; and if I had to live my life again,
> I would have made a rule to read some poetry and listen to some
> music at least once every week; for perhaps the parts of my brain
> now atrophied would thus have been kept active through use. The
> loss of these tastes is a loss of happiness, and may possibly be inju-
> rious to the intellect, and more probably to the moral character,
> by enfeebling the emotional part of our nature.

Curiously, there was one exception to this lost facility for enjoyment: "On the other hand, novels which are works of the imagination, though not of a very high order, have been for years a
wonderful relief and pleasure to me, and I often bless all novelists.
A surprising number have been read aloud to me, and I like all if
moderately good, and if they do not end unhappily—against which
a law ought to be passed."

It's hard not to see the Adler and Van Doren triptych in
place here, and in fact Darwin seems to be articulating that
distinction *avant la lettre*: perhaps as a *result* of reading so much
for information, including reading and striving to interpret
his own collections of data, he lost the ability to read for
understanding—he could no longer be moved or instructed in a
deep way by any of the arts; but he retained both the desire and

the facility for pleasure. He seems to think that such pleasure was psychically necessary to him, but he also clearly believed that the higher and more demanding arts offered possibilities of understanding that he could not acquire in any other way. Therefore he thought that his deficiency had injured him intellectually, emotionally, and perhaps even morally.

But it's also significant that Darwin believes he could have avoided his condition if he had kept in training, as it were: "perhaps the parts of my brain now atrophied would thus have been kept active through use." Darwin intuited what neuroscientists have since confirmed about the brain, that different parts of it are assigned different duties, so that his devotion to painstaking scientific research ("grinding general laws out of large collections of facts") need not have made it impossible for him to be nourished by music and poetry. He's actually a bit conflicted on this point, at first assuming that his mental habits "caused the atrophy of that part of the brain alone, on which the higher tastes depend," by some means he "cannot conceive," but the next sentence assumes that even if his habits exerted some force on the rest of his mind that force was surely not irresistible. This too has been proven correct: the plasticity of the human brain allows for major retraining, and adaptation to changing circumstances, both internal (in case of injury and disease) and external (in case of changing cognitive environments).

Darwin's account of his own history suggests that the single-minded pursuit of just one of these forms of reading can impede the others, or one of the others. Darwin read for information as well as anyone ever has, I suppose, but found that his ideal attentiveness to those texts wasn't transferable to anything demandingly artful—and yet he had no trouble reading novels. How are we to account for this?

Presumably in this way: that Darwin found novel-reading to ask, and gently ask, such a different kind of attention than he was required to give to his data that the sheer change was as good as a rest. It *was* a rest for the overworked portions of his brain. But major works of art are neither so humble nor so polite, as Auden reminds us in that passage we have already cited: "When one thinks of the attention that a great poem [or work of music] *demands....*" These demands, especially when coming at the tail end of a long workday, Darwin could not meet, and so, eventually, ceased to try: he became in this one respect "enfeebled." But he knows that *had* he tried, had he retained even a modicum of that particular variety of intellectual fitness, he would have benefited much.

I wonder if Darwin's history has a mirror image: I wonder if long-practiced contemplation of great works of literary art makes it more difficult for a person to read for information, to work methodically through textbooks and analyze data well. I am inclined to suspect that the effect is not as significant. My suspicions here derive from my own experience: I feel that my encounter with the Kindle helped restore multiple forms of readerly attentiveness. That is, not only did it restore to me the experience of being lost in a book, moving forward through the story, but that restoration in turn was transferable to my work as a scholarly pencil-in-hand reader. For me, these different forms of deep attention turned out to be mutually reinforcing; they are much more like each other than either is like, say, rapid scanning for data. I was more fortunate than Darwin—but that may be because I have never mastered any form of reading as completely as he mastered reading for information.

I am aware, however, that none of this is of any comfort, or perhaps any interest, to people who find it impossible to concentrate in *any* of these ways—people for whom textbooks, High Literature, and trashy potboilers have become pretty much equally inaccessible. I have in these recent sections outlined alternatives to the prospect of endlessly renewed distractions, brought to you via the Great Digital Skinner Box—but how many of us have a real chance of defeating those distractions? And how many of us really *want* to?

Plastic attention   ☞ As Nicholas Carr explains in his recent book *The Shallows*, the fact of neuroplasticity holds both good and bad news for the would-be reader, and the balance between the two varies according to age. After presenting a cogent outline of recent research on the brain's ability to train and retrain itself—emphasizing "the genius of our brain's construction," which is "not that it contains a lot of hardwiring but that it doesn't"*—he goes on to make this troubling point:

> Although neuroplasticity provides an escape from genetic determinism . . . it also imposes its own form of determinism on our behavior. As particular circuits in our brain strengthen through the repetition of a physical or mental activity, they begin to transform that activity into a habit. The paradox of neuroplasticity, observes [Norman] Doidge, is that, for all the mental flexibility it grants us, it can end up locking us into "rigid behaviors."

---

* Carr may overstress this point. Stanislas Dehaene's research on the brain suggests that much of the brain is significantly hardwired—and the case of Monsieur C, which I mentioned earlier, indicates that plasticity can't always overcome damage. For this reason Dehaene rarely uses the term "neuroplasticity" but speaks instead of a "neuronal recycling" hypothesis. "According to this view, human brain architecture obeys strong genetic constraints, but some circuits have evolved to tolerate a fringe of variability. Part of our visual system, for instance, is not hardwired, but remains open to changes in the environment. Within an otherwise well-structured brain, visual plasticity gave the ancient scribes the opportunity to invent reading."

The chemically triggered synapses that link our neurons program us, in effect, to want to keep exercising the circuits they've formed. Once we've wired the new circuitry in our brain, Doidge writes, "we long to keep it activated."

Plastic does not mean elastic, in other words. Our neural loops don't snap back to their former state the way a rubber band does. They hold on to their changed state. And nothing says the new state has to be a desirable one.

Thus Carr's own feeling of missing his old brain, the one that could read for long periods of time without becoming fidgety or bored. And thus the experience of people he quotes. A journalist: "I was a lit major in college, and used to be [a] voracious book reader. What happened?" A pathologist: "I can't read *War and Peace* anymore. I've lost the ability to do that. Even a blog post of more than three or four paragraphs is too much to absorb. I skim it." An English professor: "I can't get my students to read whole books anymore."

Nicholas Carr's chief emphasis in *The Shallows* is on what we lose when we exchange the patient, extended attentiveness appropriate to long-form reading for the quick skimming and sorting encouraged by the Internet; but not everyone who sees the difference feels the same way. Clay Shirky, who teaches new media at NYU, has a word of consolation for that pathologist: "no one reads *War and Peace*. It's too long, and not so interesting. The reading public has increasingly decided that Tolstoy's sacred work isn't actually worth the time it takes to read it." Shirky's view is that "the reading public" is a single, uniform entity; that it pronounces verdicts; that one of those verdicts is that long-form reading is no longer worth anyone's trouble, though apparently this did not use to be the reading public's verdict; that it's impossible to alter the public judgment or return to some *status quo ante* Internet; and that—Shirky is a self-professed "optimist"—there's no need to go back because the future will be better than the past. Don't worry, be happy. (Incidentally, or not incidentally, the reading public has chosen to pronounce this devastating verdict against Tolstoy's masterpiece by purchasing over one hundred thousand copies of the Pevear and Voloknonsky translation of *War and Peace* in the past four years. The reading public has an odd way of making its disparagement known.)

The English professor Carr quotes, N. Katherine Hayles, has a more complex—perhaps a more confused—view: in her recent work she argues, quite plausibly, that our educational models have traditionally valued what she calls "deep attention," while today's students are proficient in mobile, flexible, fast-twitch "hyper attention." Deep attention she identifies as "the cognitive style traditionally associated with the humanities" and defines it as "characterized by concentrating on a single object for long periods (say, a novel by Dickens), ignoring outside stimuli while so engaged, preferring a single information stream, and having a high tolerance for long focus times." By contrast, hyper attention requires "switching focus rapidly between different tasks, preferring multiple information streams, seeking a high level of stimulation, and having a low tolerance for boredom."

Hayles believes that "each cognitive mode has advantages and limitations. Deep attention is superb for solving complex problems represented in a single medium, but it comes at the price of environmental alertness and flexibility of response. Hyper attention excels at negotiating rapidly changing environments in which multiple foci compete for attention; its disadvantage is impatience with focusing for long periods on a non-interactive object such as a Victorian novel or complicated math problem."

She further believes that the "pedagogical challenge" for teachers, in the foreseeable future, "will be to combine hyper attention with deep attention and to cultivate both. And we can't do that if we start by stigmatizing hyper attention as inferior thinking." This sounds right to me—but if it's important to cultivate both forms of attention, and Hayles "can't get [her] students to read whole books anymore," doesn't that suggest a manifest failure of cultivation? Doesn't that indicate that the quest to maintain or preserve or simply *teach* deep attention is, in her classrooms anyway, a failure?

I think it does, and I think we cannot reasonably expect anything else. And here I am going to make what I believe to be one of the most important arguments in this book, even though it may amount to an undermining of my own profession.

Getting schooled   ☞ While virtually anyone who wants to do so can train his or her brain to the habits of long-form reading, in any given culture few people will want to. And that's to be expected. Serious "deep attention" reading has always been and will always be a minority pursuit, a fact that has been obscured by the past half-century, especially in the United States, by the dramatic increase in the percentage of the population attending college, and by the idea (only about 150 years old) that modern literature in vernacular languages should be taught at the university level.

At the beginning of the twentieth century, perhaps 2 percent of Americans attended a university; now the number is closer to 70 percent (though only about 30 percent get bachelor's degrees). A particularly sharp acceleration occurred in the years after 1945, when the GI Bill enabled soldiers returning from World War II to attend college for free, thus leading universities across the country to throw up Quonset huts for classrooms, and English professors to figure out how to teach forty students at a time, rather than eleven, how to read sonnets. (And those GIs wanted their children to have the same educational opportunities they had, or better ones.) These changes have had enormous social consequences, but for our purposes here the one that matters is this: from 1945 to 2000 or thereabouts, far more people than ever before in human history were *expected* to read, understand, appreciate, and even enjoy books.

In 2005, Wendy Griswold, Terry McDonnell, and Nathan Wright, sociologists from Northwestern University, published a paper claiming that while there was a period in which extraordinarily many Americans practiced long-form reading, whether they liked it or not, that period was indeed extraordinary and not sustainable in the long run. "We are now seeing such reading return to its former social base: a self-perpetuating minority that we shall call the reading class." I don't think of the distinction between readers and nonreaders—better, those who love reading and those who don't so much—in terms of class, which may be a function of my being a teacher of literature rather than a sociologist, but may also be a function of my knowledge that readers can be found at all social stations (witness the example of William Cobbett). But whatever designations we want to use, it has to be admitted that much of the anxiety about American reading habits, and those in other developed nations to a lesser degree, arises from frustration at not being able to sustain a permanent *expansion* of "the reading class" beyond what may be its natural limits.

The extreme reader, to coin a phrase, is a rare bird indeed. ("I have done what people do, my life makes a reasonable showing," Lynne Sharon Schwartz writes. "Can I go back to my books now?") Such people are born, not made, I think; or mostly born and only a little made. They take care of themselves; they always do go back to their books. They come out of the woodwork when Clay Shirky says that *War and Peace* isn't interesting to say that, to the contrary, it's *immensely* interesting, fascinating, absorbing, and by the way, Mr. Shirky, have you ever *tried* reading it or are you speaking out of ignorance?— and then back to their books they go. Those are my tribe, but they are few. It is more common to come across the person who has known the joys of reading but who can be distracted from them: people who, rather like Nicholas Carr, once had a smoothly functioning reading brain but allowed it to fall into disrepair. It is for such people that I have written this book. But even these folks are never more than a small percentage of the population.

American universities are largely populated by people who don't fit either of these categories—often really smart people, like the Florida State student Joe O'Shea, but ones for whom the prospect of several hours attending to words on pages (pages of a single text) is not attractive. For lovers of books and reading, and especially for those of us who become teachers, this fact can be painful and frustrating. We love reading, we think it's wonderful, and we want other people to think so too. "What we have loved, / Others will love," wrote Wordsworth, "and we will teach them how." A noble sentiment! Inspiring! But what if after great labor we discover—this often happens—that we *can't* teach them how? Whose fault is that?

Perhaps it isn't anyone's fault. Early in this book I cited Steven Pinker's comment that "Children are wired for sound, but print is an optional accessory that must be painstakingly bolted on." The key here is "painstakingly": there can be many pains, in multiple senses of the word, for all parties involved, and it cannot be surprising that many of the recipients of the bolting aren't overly appreciative, and that even those who *are* appreciative don't find the procedure notably pleasant. Thus my efforts throughout this

book to dissociate reading from academic life, not just because
teachers and professors make reading so much more dutiful and
good-for-you than it ought to be but also because the whole
environment of *school* is simply alien to what long-form reading
has been for almost all of its history.

Rarely has education been about teaching children, adolescents,
or young adults how to read lengthy and complicated texts with
sustained, deep, *appreciative* attention—at least, not since the invention of the printing press. When books were scarce the situation
was different: the North African boy who later became known
to history as St. Augustine spent countless hours of his education
poring over, analyzing word-by-word, and memorizing a handful of
books, most of them by Virgil and Cicero; this model was followed
largely because no one *had* many books, so each one was treated as
precious. Augustine's biographer Peter Brown has commented that
some of Augustine's intellectual eccentricities are the product of "a
mind steeped too long in too few books"—something that can be
said of almost nobody today.

Even after Gutenberg this assumption of scarcity persisted, as
George Steiner has noted in an anecdote about one of the leading scholars of the Renaissance: "The tale is told of how Erasmus,
walking home on a foul night, glimpsed a tiny fragment of print in
the mire. He bent down, seized upon it and lifted it to a flickering
light with a cry of thankful joy. Here was a miracle."

But as the historian Ann Blair explains, the printing press
ushered in an age of information overload. In the seventeenth century one French scholar cried out, "We have reason to fear that the
multitude of books which grows every day in a prodigious fashion
will make the following centuries fall into a state as barbarous as
that of the centuries that followed the fall of the Roman Empire."
Such will be our fate "unless we try to prevent this danger by
separating those books which we must throw out or leave in

oblivion from those which one should save and within the latter between what is useful and what is not."* So what did those poor deluged people do? Well, they adopted several strategies. First, they practiced various ways of marking important passages in books: with special symbols, with slips of paper, and so on. (Several of the annotative strategies mentioned earlier have their origins in this period.) Then they came up with various ways of organizing books: there were now so many that figuring out how to arrange them became quite a puzzle, so the learned began debates on this subject that would culminate in the creation of the great Dewey Decimal Classification.

One of the most widely quoted sentences of Sir Francis Bacon—it comes from his essay "Of Studies"—concerns the reading of books: "Some books are to be tasted, others to be swallowed and some few to be chewed and digested; that is, some books are to be read only in parts; others to be read, but not curiously; and some few to be read wholly, and with diligence and attention." This is usually taken as a wise or sententious general comment about the worthiness of various texts, but Ann Blair shows that Bacon was making a very practical recommendation to people who were overwhelmed by the availability of books and

---

* Blair shows that such alarm was quite common, and indeed can be found in various periods going back to the high Middle Ages, a period which by our standards and even the standards of the sixteenth century had few books. For instance, in the thirteenth century we hear from Vincent of Beauvais: "Since the multitude of books, the shortness of time and the slipperiness of memory do not allow all things which are written to be equally retained in the mind, I decided to reduce in one volume in a compendium and in summary order some flowers selected according to my talents from all the authors I was able to read"—that is, a kind of Culture's Greatest Hits. But after the invention of the printing press, books had so multiplied that a project like Vincent's would have been self-evidently absurd.

couldn't imagine how they were going to read them all. Bacon
tells such worried folks that they *can't* read them all, and so should
develop strategies of discernment that enable them to make wise
decisions about how to invest their time. I think Bacon would
have applauded Clay Shirky's comment that we suffer not from
"information overload" but from "filter failure." Bacon's famous
sentence is really a strategy for filtering.

Blair also points out that certain enterprising scholars recognized that this information overload created a market for reference
works and books that claimed to summarize important texts—We
read the books so you don't have to!—or promised to teach tech-
niques for the rapid assimilation of knowledge. But serious scholars like Meric Casaubon denounced the search for "a shorter way"
to learning, insisting that "the best method to learning . . . is inde-
fatigable (soe farr as the bodie will beare) industrie, and assiduitie,
in reading good authors, such as have had the approbation of all
learned ages." No shortcuts allowed.

All this should sound familiar: Casaubon might be a professor
today warning students against Wikipedia, and it turns out that
every era has its intellectual hucksters willing to sell knowledge
on the cheap to the panicky or lazy. But perhaps especially noteworthy is Bacon's acknowledgment that there is a place for what
Katherine Hayles would call "hyper attention" as well as "deep
attention." Some books don't need to be read with the patience
and care I have been recommending here; at times it's okay, even
necessary, to skim (merely to "taste" rather than to ruminate).
And as Shreeharsh Kelkar has pointed out, "To be successful today,
it not only becomes necessary to skim but it becomes essential to
skim well."

Except in those cultures in which books have been scarce, like
Augustine's Roman North Africa, the aims of education have often
focused, though rarely explicitly so, on the skills of skimming well.

Peter Norvig says, "When the only information on the topic is a handful of essays or books, the best strategy is to read these works with total concentration. But when you have access to thousands of articles, blogs, videos, and people with expertise on the topic, a good strategy is to skim first to get an overview. Skimming and concentrating can and should coexist." Norvig is Research Director at Google, so he might be expected to say something like this, but I still think he's right—except, I would argue, concentrating has rarely received equal billing with skimming.

Rarely have young people been expected to have truly deep knowledge of particular texts. Instead, education, especially in its "liberal arts" embodiments, has been devoted to providing students with *navigational* tools—with enough knowledge to find their way through situations that they might confront later in life. (Even the old English public schools flogged their students through years of Latin and Greek not because Latin and Greek were intrinsically valuable, still less useful, but because the *discipline* of such study would have a salutary effect on young men's characters. And these are the terms in which survivors of that system typically praise it.) This is one of the ways in which the *artes liberales* are supposed to be "liberal," that is, "liberating": they free you to make your own way through the challenges of life without requiring external props.*

---

*For John Milton, in the seventeenth century, education was primarily meant to be liberating in a different sense: to free us from bondage to sin, which afflicts all human beings since Adam and Eve sinned in the Garden of Eden. "The end then of Learning is to repair the ruins of our first Parents by regaining to know God aright, and out of that knowledge to love him, to imitate him, to be like him, as we may the nearest by possessing our souls of true virtue, which being united to the heavenly grace of faith makes up the highest perfection."

Reading Milton's treatise "Of Education," one doesn't know whether or not to laugh. Here's a tiny part of his plan for young men's studies: "And having thus past

All this to say that the idea that many teachers hold today that one of the purposes of education is to teach students to love reading—or at least to appreciate and enjoy whole books—is largely alien to the history of education. And perhaps alien to the history of reading as well: a chief theme of Jonathan Rose's magisterial *Intellectual Life of the British Working Classes* is that the culture of reading among those classes was more dynamic, more impassioned, *before* the study of English literature was incorporated into the general curriculum of English schools (in the wake of the Education Act of 1870). Rose's book is largely a celebration of autodidacticism, of people whose reading—and especially the reading of classic texts, from Homer to Dante to Shakespeare to the great Romantic poets—wasn't imposed on them by anyone, and who often had to overcome significant social obstacles in order to read. "The autodidacts' mission statement," Rose writes, was "to be more

---

the principles of Arithmetic, Geometry, Astronomy, and Geography with a general compact of Physics, they may descend in Mathematics to the instrumental science of Trigonometry, and from thence to Fortification, Architecture, Enginry, or Navigation. And in natural Philosophy they may proceed leisurely from the History of Meteors, Minerals, plants and living Creatures as far as Anatomy. Then also in course might be read to them out of some not tedious Writer the Institution of Physic." It's hard not to think that Milton is deliberately sketching an impossible ideal, as Thomas More does in *Utopia*, or as R. A. Lafferty does in "The Primary Education of the Camiroi." But even if so, it's noteworthy that Milton places no emphasis on his students' learning to appreciate, still less to love, the objects of their study. Rather, the end of all this instruction, beyond its spiritual function, is eminently practical: "I call therefore a complete and generous Education that which fits a man to perform justly, skillfully and magnanimously all the offices both private and public of Peace and War."

Milton also believed that, if his program were fully and properly implemented, even the laziest student would find his studies utterly delightful.

than passive consumers of literature, to be active thinkers and writers. Those who proclaimed that 'knowledge is power' meant that the only true education is self-education, and they often regarded the expansion of formal educational opportunities with suspicion." The academic study of literature is a wonderful thing, and not just because it has paid my salary for most of my adult life, but it is not an unmixed blessing, and teachers will rarely find it possible simply to inculcate the practices of deeply attentive reading that I commend in this book.

Over the past hundred and fifty years, it has become increasingly difficult to extricate reading from academic expectations; but I believe that such extrication is necessary. Education is and should be primarily about intellectual navigation, about—I scruple not to say it—skimming well, and reading carefully for information in order to upload content. Slow and patient reading, by contrast, properly belongs to our leisure hours.

Yes, I know that the word "school" derives from *scholia*, meaning leisure. I have tried that one on my students, with no more success than anyone else who has ever tried that one on students. When we say that education is a leisure activity, we simply mean that you can only pursue education if you are temporarily freed from the responsibility of providing yourself with food and shelter. Maybe this freedom comes from your parents; maybe it comes from loans that you're going to devote a good many years to repaying. But *somebody* is buying you time to read, think, and study. This is not just a legitimate but a vital point, one that every student really should remember.* But it can only be misleading and

---

*Though the situation is rather more complicated for those who work to pay their way through school, and therefore try to do both full-time or nearly full-time, as I well know, having once been such a student.

frustrating—trust me, I've learned from experience—to call this
leisure, because leisure for us has come to mean "what we do in our
spare time simply because we want to"—what we do at whim, one
might say, or even at Whim, as Randall Jarrell's critic friend read
Kim, "just because he liked to, wanted to, couldn't help himself."
From this kind of leisurely encounter, education, however wonderful, must be distinguished.

There is a kind of attentiveness proper to school, to purpose-
ful learning of all kinds, but in general it is closer to "hyper
attention" than to "deep attention." I would argue that even
reading for information—reading textbooks and the like—does
not require extended unbroken focus. It requires discipline but
not raptness, I think: the crammer chains himself to the textbook because of time pressures, not because the book itself
requires unbroken concentration. Given world enough and time,
the harried student could read for a while, do something else,
come back and refresh his memory, take another break . . . but
the reader of even the most intellectually demanding work of
literary art would lose a great deal by following such tactics.
No novel or play or long poem will offer its full rewards to
someone who consumes it in small chunks and crumbs. The
attention it demands is the deep kind.

I am not at all sure that deep attention to anything in particular
can be taught in a straightforward way: it is intimately associated
with what Auden calls "that eye-on-the-object" look, and may,
perhaps, only arise from within, according to some inexplicable
internal necessity of being. Some people—many people—most
people—will not experience that internal necessity of being in
books, in texts; "a cook mixing a sauce" finds it elsewhere, as does
the "flaker of flints" who forgets his dinner. But for people like
Erasmus (with his "cry of thankful joy" on spying a fragment of
print) or Lynne Sharon Schwartz ("Can I get back to my books

now?"), books are the natural and inevitable and permanent means of being absorbed in something other than the self.

But then there are the people Nicholas Carr interviewed, and Carr himself: people who know what it is like to be lost in a book, who value that experience, but who have misplaced it—who can't get back, as Lucy Pevensie for a time can't get back to Narnia: what was an opening to another world is now the flat planked back of a wardrobe. They're the ones who need help, and want it, and are prepared to receive it. I had become one of those people myself, or was well on my way to it, when I was rescued through the novelty of reading on a Kindle. My hyper-attentive habits were alienating me further and further from the much older and (one would have thought) more firmly established habits of deep attention. I was rapidly becoming a victim of my own mind's plasticity, until a new technology helped me to remember how to do something that for years had been instinctive, unconscious, natural. I don't know whether an adult who has *never* practiced deep attention—who has never seriously read for information *or* for understanding, or even for delight—can learn how. But I'm confident that anyone who has ever had this facility can recover it: they just have to want that recovery enough to make sacrifices for it, something they will only do if they can vividly *recall* what that experience was like.

Quiet, please ☞ But how can we concentrate, how can we cultivate or practice deep attention, how can we *read* with all this *noise*? Impediments surround us, even when we're away from our screens. In explaining why he wrote his book *In Pursuit of Silence*, George Prochnik offers a telling statement: "I've always been a lover of silence, and this love is bound up with my passion for books. The writer Stefan Zweig once defined a book as a 'handful

of silence that assuages torment and unrest.' For years before
I began writing about the subject, I'd been feeling that silence was
a diminishing natural resource. I wanted to understand whether
this was more than a subjective impression. If so, why had the
world become louder, and what could be done to reinstate silence
as a value in our culture?" For Prochnik, then, the constancy of the
sheer racket in our culture is a threat centrally, if not primarily, to
books and reading. Zweig's "handful of silence" slips through our
hands when our ears are too frequently and too harshly assaulted.

But for the reader, it has always been thus. In *The Intellectual Life
of the British Working Classes*, Jonathan Rose describes the difficulties that intellectually ambitious workers (or children of workers)
invariably had even in finding somewhere to set their books; and
if they achieved that, what then? Rose cites the case of Dennis
Marsden, who grew up during the years of World War II and
whose parents had serious academic ambitions for him—but how
was he to pursue them in their tiny cramped home? Years afterward Marsden described his situation:

> Should the wireless be on or off? Could the younger children play
> noisily? Could the father stretch his legs and tell the day's tales?
> To ask for silence here was to offend the life of the family, was to
> go against it in its natural moments of coming together, of relax-
> ation. So many [scholarship boys from poor families] learned the
> early habit of working with the wireless on and the family talking,
> of building a cone of silence around themselves.

So it often must be, then, now, and in the future: we readers must
learn to build our own "cone of silence"; the world won't do it for us.

Our first experiences with books (texts) are mediated by the
voices of others: someone reads a story to us, often while sitting
beside us—a significant point. Our visual attention is directed to

the book itself, because of the pictures, of course, but this has the added effect of teaching us to be attentive to pages. We learn the *posture* proper to our dealings with books; we also learn to absorb knowledge through our ears while absorbing other, but related, knowledge through our eyes. This is rather different from watching a storyteller in action, when hearing and listening are directed to the same source. (The boy I saw on the Vancouver ferry listening to his father read Harry Potter assumed what is for many people an unusual posture: facing the person reading to him. In households where parents continue past the stage of picture books to read to their children this happens regularly; but there aren't so many of those anymore.) To sit next to an adult who reads to you while turning the pages—who points to certain images from time to time and perhaps, later, to certain words—is, in our culture and many others, to occupy an important transitional stage. It is a move toward drawing meaning and value from a page of writing; it is a move toward silence.

One of the most hotly debated topics among historians of reading involves the rise of silent reading. In a famous passage in the *Confessions*, Augustine describes visiting Ambrose, Bishop of Milan, in the great man's chambers, only to find him casting his eyes across the page without making a sound or even moving his lips. That Augustine found this behavior so noteworthy, and explained it in such detail, has often been taken as an indication that Augustine was unfamiliar with silent reading; Augustine's account is regularly cited as evidence that people started reading aloud only at some later date.

But the eminent classicist Bernard Knox has shown that that's too facile an interpretation: he calls attention to passages from plays by Euripides and Aristophanes, eight hundred years before Augustine, in which characters are clearly reading silently on stage. In the latter case it's the source of laughs: one man while reading silently tells another to pour him a cup of wine, and the straight man replies, "Does it really say *that*?" This could only work dramatically if silent reading is something familiar to the audience.

More recently, though, Paul Saenger has argued that the lack not only of punctuation but even of spaces between words in ancient texts—the first line of the *Iliad* would have looked something like this: RAGEGODDESSSINGTHERAGEOFPELEUSSONACHILLES— made silent reading utterly impractical: when confronted with such rammed-together symbols the reader has no choice but to sound the text out, if only in an undertone. (You may have done just that when you encountered that line.) But, other scholars have retorted, just because we who are unused to reading such texts can't do it doesn't mean that those who spent a lifetime reading that way would be equally flummoxed.

The question is vexed, and continues to be vexed in later periods. Saenger believes that Irish monks started creating manuscripts with spaces between words in the late seventh century—spurred to do so, he contends, by the monastic commitment to silence— and that the practice spread across Europe in the next few centuries, leading to silent reading becoming the universal norm in monasteries. Yet in the *Didascalicon* Hugh seems to assume that a key element of the practice of *ruminatio* is the repeated murmuring of the text one is meditating on.

I do not know how to resolve these historical questions, but this much is clear: the more noise surrounds us, the harder it is to read aloud. Reading aloud, and still more *murmured* reading, requires a quiet enough environment that you can hear what you speak; otherwise it is a pointless activity. And it might be worth pausing here to note that city life has *always* been loud—that is not an artifact of modern times. Bruce R. Smith's extraordinary study *The Acoustic World of Early Modern England* gives us a full and rather disorienting sense of just how cacophonous the world was for many of our ancestors half-a-millennium ago. And Diana Webb in her book *Privacy and Solitude in the Middle Ages* argues, convincingly, that many people, men and women alike, sought monastic life less from piety than from a desperate need to find refuge from all the racket. Maybe they just wanted to find a place where they could be left alone to read.

The simple conclusion we may draw from all this is: the noisier the environment, the more readers are driven to be silent. It is only in "privacy and solitude" that reading aloud or murmuring can ever be a reasonable option and rarely have our ancestors had that option. The boy trying to study at the kitchen table while the clamor of family life goes on around him is a typical figure in the history of reading. No one could plausibly claim that we late moderns are uniquely challenged in this respect: surely a higher percentage of human beings today have regular access to silence than at any time in human history. Most Americans and Western Europeans, and many people elsewhere—not all, mind you—live in environments with quiet rooms, or quiet corners. And many who lack quiet homes have had access to libraries, which have for centuries been dedicated, as it were, to silence.

That may be changing, though. Here's an example from the United Kingdom that has analogues in several other countries. In 2008, when Andy Burnham was Gordon Brown's Secretary of State for Culture, Media and Sport, he announced that libraries had to change: "Libraries should be a place for families and joy and chatter. The word chatter might strike fear into the heart of traditionalists but libraries should be social places that offer an antidote to the isolation of someone playing on the internet at home." Libraries need to "look beyond the bookcase," which means, among other things, allowing the use of cellphones and selling (or at least allowing people to bring in) food and drink.

Even among educated folk, these proposals got some support, largely out of fear that without some such change libraries will become irrelevant and unused, and eventually will disappear altogether. But others fumed. Victoria Coren wrote, "My brain is struggling with the philosophical question (like that of the tree falling in the empty forest): if there is nothing inside but people eating burgers and playing the Sims, is it actually a library? Isn't it just an internet cafe?" To the "they must look beyond the bookcase" line, Coren retorted, "Why? Why must they? They're libraries. The bookcase is exactly where they should be looking. For God's sake, someone should be. I can eat and make phone calls at home."

Similarly, Charlotte Leslie wrote, "The tragedy of all this is that the 'chatter' that Burnham wants to bring into our libraries is already available in coffee shops and in many bookshops." What's missing, for many people, is a place of quiet. "The well-off will still be able to access silence—for example in a room of their spacious detached house, or their country escape." But Leslie's local libraries "are often peopled with . . . students who can't find a quiet place at home to work. . . . Denying these children the space and silence to study and contemplate the past that the better-off may be able to find in a spare room of their house is nothing short of social discrimination at its worst." Leslie fears a return to a time "when only the elite could afford silence."

Perhaps the most curious aspect of Burnham's proposal is this: his chief worry is that someone is doing something alone at home, and libraries need to be alternatives to that. Yes, his chosen example is someone playing video games, but for Burnham, playing video games is bad because it tends to involve "isolation."

Well, if it comes to that, reading tends to be considerably more isolating, in Burnham's sense of the word, than playing video games. Many people play video games with others, either friends in the room with them or online opponents and allies. They might even talk on the phone while playing, perhaps to friends who are engaged in the same game. You can't do any of that with a book, at least not while you're reading it. Reading is a greater offender against sociability than gaming. It would be perfectly consistent with Burnham's stated views to say that we need libraries in order to draw people away from the disabling solitude of reading.

We all find our enemies in different places, I suppose, but Burnham seems to have found an odd one. Solitude may be more accessible for modern Westerners than for anyone else in history, but it would be perverse to say that we have too much of it. Or why would so many people complain, as we saw at the beginning of this book, of their seemingly infinite capacity for distraction *from* solitude by the multiple varieties of media, and especially social media?

As I was in the midst of writing this section I came across an illuminating essay (indeed, I was almost certainly distracted from writing by the arrival of some new items in my RSS reader) by Paul Bloom, a psychologist at Yale University. Bloom begins by asking and then answering the question, "How do Americans spend their leisure time?"

> Our main leisure activity is, by a long shot, participating in experiences that we know are not real. When we are free to do whatever we want, we retreat to the imagination—to worlds created by others, as with books, movies, video games, and television (over four hours a day for the average American), or to worlds we ourselves create, as when daydreaming and fantasizing. While citizens of other countries might watch less television, studies in England and the rest of Europe find a similar obsession with the unreal.

How to explain this "obsession"? "One solution to this puzzle," and one that Bloom largely agrees with, "is that the pleasures of the imagination exist because they hijack mental systems that have evolved for real-world pleasure. We enjoy imaginative experiences because at some level we don't distinguish them from real ones." Thus the power, as Bloom goes on to say, of fiction: the whole world wept over the death of Little Nell in Dickens's *The Old Curiosity Shop*,* and before the final Harry Potter book appeared J. K. Rowling got countless letters from fans pleading with her not to kill off Harry (or any other particularly beloved character).

Though Bloom does not cite it in his essay, recent research confirms that something extraordinary happens in our brains when we read stories. Nicholas Carr describes it in *The Shallows*: "Researchers used brain scans to examine what happens inside people's heads as they read fiction. They found that 'readers mentally simulate each new situation encountered in a narrative.' . . . The brain regions that are activated 'closely mirror those involved when people perform, imagine, or observe similar real-world activities.'"

With this research in mind, it's important to circle back to something Paul Bloom notes: "We enjoy imaginative experiences because at some level we don't distinguish them from real ones"— not that we *can't* distinguish them, but that we *don't*. Bloom points out that while very small children may be confused in these matters, well before the age of four they have it all scoped out pretty accurately: "Two-year-olds pretend to be animals and airplanes, and they can understand when other people do the same thing. A child sees her father roaring and prowling like a lion, and might run away, but she doesn't act as though she thinks her father is actually a lion. If she believed that, she would be terrified." And yet

---

* Except for Oscar Wilde, who famously said that "One must have a heart of stone to read the death of Little Nell without laughing."

that two-year-old utters some pretty convincing screams, and her heart races; if it weren't for the smile on her face we might think she really *is* frightened.

There was a time when I read Harry Potter books to my son, too, and—do I need to call out "SPOILER ALERT" here?—I well recall the look on his face when, at the end of *Goblet of Fire*, Voldemort kills Cedric Diggory. I think he saw that moment as vividly as Harry did. And yet Coleridge was right when he wrote about that readerly necessity called the "willing suspension of disbe-lief": we have to *consent* to the partial dissolution of the boundaries between the imagined and the real, and, I think, *learn* how to make that consent effectual. For some of us, it becomes deeply habitual, but the spell of reading is always in danger of being broken: What if the phone had started ringing as I read to Wes of Harry's encounter with the Dark Lord? What if I had commenced a sneezing fit? What if I had started giggling? All these would have, to varying degrees and varying ways, broken the spell and undone the consent. Disbelief would have reclaimed its usual throne.

When engaged in imaginative play, we don't like it when disenchantment threatens. At a particularly intense point in the video game, the player hangs up the phone or shushes the friend next to him on the sofa. He builds or rebuilds for himself a "cone of silence," like the boy studying at the dinner table, or like the absorbed reader in the café who doesn't notice that the server has just asked if she wants another cup of coffee. And noting all this we may at long last be able to answer, or begin to answer, a question I posed long ago: Why are we even taken by the whim to read? People who have had this kind of experience will want to have it again and again; and for some of us it happens most powerfully through the written word.

Such imaginative engagement can only come through the written word when the reader possesses, or is possessed by, deep solitude—whether that solitude is given by circumstance or created, even in the midst of a crowd, by force of will sharpened by habit. The video game presses itself upon your attention, it constantly confronts you with stimuli to which some response is required; but books do not work that way. As Olaudah Equiano discovered, when you put your ear to the book it remains silent. You have to continue to throw yourself into it. This is something easy to learn: children are quite good at it, as Elizabeth Bowen notes: "At any age, the reader must come *across*: the child reader is the most eager and quick to do so; he not only lends to the story, he flings into the story the whole of his sensuous experience which from being limited is the more intense." But what is easy to learn may be hard to sustain. Pascal in his *Pensées* notes that "the error of Stoicism" is to believe you can do always what you can do sometimes.

"The reader must come *across*"—this is the key, this is why the reader can't do without solitude and concentration. The effort has manifold rewards, but effort is required. It is lessened by habit, but never eliminated; and attentiveness remains always an achievement, one that cannot be taken for granted. Yet when it happens, it can happen powerfully. "I can always tell when you're reading somewhere in the house," Francis Spufford's mother used to say to him when he was a child. "There's a special silence, a *reading* silence."

Once more, with feeling   ☞ I read Tolstoy's *Anna Karenina* for the first time when I was in graduate school and came back to it about a decade later when I taught a course in the history of the novel. A few more years passed before I taught that course again, and when I did one passage from the book struck me with exceptional force—all the more exceptional because I had never really noticed it before. In fact, I could not remember having read it at all.

When Levin and Kitty have their first child, a son, Levin is nonplussed by his own reaction to the red, wrinkled little thing: "This beautiful baby inspired only a feeling of squeamishness and pity in him." Only when the baby sneezes does he feel, inexplicably, a sense of pride. He remains deeply uneasy:

> What he felt for this small being was not at all what he had expected. There was nothing happy or joyful in this feeling; on the contrary, there was a new tormenting fear. There was an awareness of a new region of vulnerability. And this awareness was so tormenting at first, the fear lest this helpless being should suffer was so strong, that because of it he scarcely noticed the strange feeling of senseless joy and even pride he had experienced when the baby sneezed.

Reading this passage on my third time through the book, this passage I had never noticed before, tears came to my eyes. A few months earlier my own son had been born, and I recognized Levin's feeling—that "vulnerability" of knowing that from now on this small person's suffering would be my suffering too.

That was a simple and straightforward transformation of readerly experience: I once was blind, but then I saw. Yet changes in our responses to books can be subtler, more complex, and harder to understand.

Those of us who pride ourselves on catholicity of literary taste find it difficult to admit that our range of appreciation has limits. But for many years I just couldn't enjoy G. K. Chesterton, no matter how hard I tried. This troubled me, because some writers whom I very much respect are themselves devoted to Chesterton. I think particularly of C. S. Lewis, whose style has some distinctly Chestertonian elements. But what in Lewis I found charming,

in Chesterton himself I found infuriating. I read book after book
of Chesterton's trying to find a key that would unlock his appeal;
I kept going, I think, because I often felt that something was eventually going to click. It was like trying to pick out a single voice in
a noisy room: you think that any moment now you'll get it, you'll
isolate it and will be able to lock your attention upon it.

This process went on for some years, in part because I needed
to teach Chesterton in one of my classes. The book I normally
used was his novel *The Man Who Was Thursday*, which at least had
never annoyed me, even if it hadn't yielded me much pleasure.
And then one year when I was rereading the book in prepara-
tion for that class—I did this with some care every time I taught
because nothing in it had ever remained vividly in my mind—
something clicked in my brain. The book *grasped* me, held me.
I read now not with dutiful care but with absolute delight, and it
felt to me that I had never read it at all. I knew what was coming
and yet, somehow, had no idea what was coming. *The Man Who
Was Thursday* became, and I suspect will always remain, one of my
favorite books.

My attitude toward the rest of Chesterton's writings changed
too, though not completely. What had annoyed me utterly, primarily
Chesterton's overuse of paradox, now annoyed me somewhat; I was
not blind to the faults of his writing, but the faults no longer blinded
me to the virtues. A general frustration—once, years ago, I opened
my back door and *threw* Chesterton's biography of Francis of Assisi
as far as I could—became a somewhat qualified appreciation, an
appreciation now always accompanied by affection.

This sudden and dramatic change is inexplicable to me.
Whereas my encounter with *Anna Karenina*—or rather with one
particular scene in *Anna Karenina*—altered because my circumstances altered, nothing happened in my life that would account
for my sudden love for *The Man Who Was Thursday*. I do not believe

I underwent any significant mental changes either. All I can say is: for a long time I didn't get it, and then I got it.

Such is the mystery of rereading, and few topics are more important for anyone who wants to make sense, and make *value*, of reading. If most of us read too fast, most of us also read too many books and are unwisely reluctant to return to something we think we already know. I use "think" there advisedly, because as my examples show, a first encounter with a worthwhile book is never a complete encounter, and we are usually in error to make it a final one. But those who want to have read, who are checking books off their "bucket list," will find the thought of rereading even more repulsive than the thought of reading slowly and ruminatively. And yet rereading a book can often be a more significant, dramatic, and, yes, *new* experience than encountering an unfamiliar work.

W. H. Auden's history with Kierkegaard was something like the opposite of mine with Chesterton. Late in his life he attempted to make sense of his responses to Kierkegaard over a period of thirty years:

> Like Pascal, Nietzsche, and Simone Weil, Kierkegaard is one of those writers whom it is very difficult to estimate justly. When one reads them for the first time, one is bowled over by their original-ity (they speak in a voice one has never heard before) and by the sharpness of their insights (they say things which no one before them has said, and which, henceforward, no reader will ever for-get). But with successive readings one's doubts grow, one begins to react against their overemphasis on one aspect of the truth at the expense of all the others, and one's first enthusiasm may all too easily turn into an equally exaggerated aversion.

In a book I wrote some years ago, I cited this passage in commending Auden as an exemplar of "charitable reading." Further

reflection eventually led Auden to see Kierkegaard's limitations as
a thinker, but he knew that it would not be fair to Kierkegaard, *or
to his own younger self*, to allow his "first enthusiasm [to] turn into an
equally exaggerated aversion." (I had just this lesson in mind when
I said earlier that I do not think my current discomfort with the
style of *Absalom, Absalom!* simply trumps my twenty-year-old self's
love of that book.)

Rereading Kierkegaard was vital for Auden because it
was simultaneously a testing of Kierkegaard's wisdom and
a self-testing. Precisely because Kierkegaard had been so
important to him, had "bowled him over," had influenced his
thoughts and acts—Kierkegaard had been instrumental to
Auden's embrace of Christianity—it was necessary to revisit
his work. And that revisiting would be an exercise in active
memory: Auden would re-encounter Kierkegaard's words and
also his own earlier responses as a reader. It's a kind of intellectual parallax or binocular vision: by comparing his response
at age sixty to his response at age thirty, Auden could learn
something about how far his own thought had come, and what
his other reading and other experiences had taught him along
the way.

The poet L. E. Sissman offers this evocative image:

A list of books that you reread is like a clearing in the forest: a
level, clean, well-lighted place where you set down your burdens
and set up your home, your identity, your concerns, your continuity in a world that is at best indifferent, at worst malign. Since
you, the reader, are that hero of modern literature, the existential
loner, the smallest denominator of moral force, it behooves you
to take counsel, sustenance, and solace from the writers who have
been writing about you these hundred or five hundred years, to
sequester yourself with their books and read and reread them to

get a fix on yourself and a purchase on the world that will, with luck, like the house in the clearing, last you for life.

Sissman is one of those who sees the most important books as sources of wisdom—of *counsel*, as Walter Benjamin, a similar kind of reader, put it.* They have a word for you, as the saying goes, which is why Sissman declares that they "have been writing about you" for all these centuries and that revisiting them helps you to "get a fix on yourself," as well as "a purchase on the world."

I mentioned early in this book the kind of rereading distinctive to the *fan*—the Tolkien addict, say, or the devotee of Jane Austen or Trollope or the Harry Potter books. The return to such books is often motivated by a desire to dwell for a time in a self-contained fictional universe, with its own boundaries and its own rules. (It is a moot question whether Austen and Trollope's first readers were drawn to their novels for these reasons, but their readers today often are.) Such rereading is not purely a matter of escapism, even though that is one reason for its attraction: we should note that it's not what readers are escaping *from* but what they are escaping *into* that counts most. Most of us do not find fictional

---

*From Benjamin's profound essay "The Storyteller": "All this points to the nature of every real story. It contains, openly or covertly, something useful. The usefulness may, in one case, consist in a moral; in another, in some practical advice; in a third, in a proverb or maxim. In every case the storyteller is a man who has counsel for his readers. But if today 'having counsel' is beginning to have an old-fashioned ring, this is because the communicability of experience is decreasing. In consequence we have no counsel either for ourselves or for others. After all, counsel is less an answer to a question than a proposal concerning the continuation of a story which is just unfolding. To seek this counsel one would first have to be able to tell the story. (Quite apart from the fact that a man is receptive to counsel only to the extent that he allows his situation to speak.) Counsel woven into the fabric of real life is wisdom."

worlds appealing because we find our own lives despicable, though censorious people often make that assumption. Auden once wrote that "there must always be . . . escape-art, for man needs escape as he needs food and deep sleep." The sleeper does not disdain consciousness.

But in any event this is not the only kind of rereading. I vividly remember when and from whom I first learned that it was acceptable to read a book more than once: Irene Hendricks, my English teacher in my junior year of high school, opened this door for me. Mrs. Hendricks was a very large woman who as she taught sat on a kind of high stool behind a lectern; she had a wandering eye, but it was hard to tell which one wandered, so that you could never be sure whether she was looking at you or not. This added, somehow, to her air of authority, so I was inclined to listen when she stated one day that she read Proust's *Remembrance of Things Past* (as it was then called) every summer.

I was quite taken by this remark. I was an avid reader and had reread several books, but always with guilt: though not a dedicated student, I had just enough Richard Rodriguez in me to keep track of my reading and to feel that I should always be reading something new. I kept a list of favorite books and when I read a new one I liked, would gravely consider—taking due account of the dangers of momentary enthusiasm—whether it deserved a place on that list. At that age I would have been an absolute sucker for any authoritative register of Books One Must Read, and I thank God that I never came across any of them. And the idea of having a *settled practice* of returning to the same book each summer befuddled me. But Mrs. Hendricks said that she did so because the book was so great, and so deep, and so subtle that she always found something new in it, always had more to learn about it and through it.

When I discovered, some weeks later, that *Remembrance of Things Past* was not one book but six, and six hefty ones at that,

I didn't know what to think. On the one hand, it made more sense
to revisit something of that size than to revisit the two-hundred
pagers in which I specialized at the time; on the other hand, I
wondered why anyone would sacrifice such a big chunk of every
summer to the same work—because it would certainly *require*
a big chunk. (Only years later did I begin to wonder whether
Mrs. Hendricks had been wholly truthful in her claim. At the time
my trust in her was absolute.) My only absolute conviction in the
matter was that I had no intention of reading Proust myself.

But I remembered Mrs. Hendricks's claim so vividly because
of its implicit suggestion that some books hold more value, more
counsel perhaps, or simple insight, than we can receive at a single
reading. When I had reread in the past, it had been a fan's act,
prompted by an unrealizable desire to recapture an experience:
my favorite book at the time was Arthur C. Clarke's *Childhood's
End*, and it was not possible for me to feel again what I felt when I
first read of the Overlords' shocking emergence from their ships,
their coming among us. (And despite the many failings of memory,
I recall that moment still, and so to this day could not renew my
first encounter with Clarke's novel, even if I could return somehow to the emotional receptiveness of my fifteen-year-old self.)
But Mrs. Hendricks was choosing to reread Proust for reasons that
transcended anything I then knew. I thought people only read the
Bible that way.

All of this suggests that rereading can be a product not of
simple dissatisfaction, nor of the fan's utter enchantment, but
rather of some curious mix of gratification and a feeling of
incompletion. You can reread not from love or hatred but from a
sense, often inchoate, that there's more to this book than you have
yet been able to receive. This may happen because the book isn't
meant to be "reaped in a single traverse," to reborrow a phrase
from Hugh Kenner, or because when you first read the book you

weren't fully equipped for its challenge, whether because of your stage of life or your (temporary) state of mind. That voice in your head—think of it as the voice of Mrs. Hendricks, whose minatory eye may or may not be upon you—that tells you to pick it up and read it again is a voice whose counsel for you should be heeded. You just have to practice to hear it above all those other voices screaming for novelty.

Judge, jury, executioner ☞ When we read, and after we read, we judge. And certainly *before* we read: we can only have a whim to read something because we've made some kind of prejudgment in its favor, perhaps because of its author or genre, perhaps because of a review or the recommendation of a friend. Such prejudgments are always revisable, and in fact our comments about a book are quite often expressions of such revision: "I was really disappointed" or "It was a lot better than I expected." And rereading, when it's voluntary anyway, always marks a presumption in favor of a book, even if the presumption is only "Surely you can't be as bad as I thought you were the first time around."

Critical reflection of some kind is inevitable, so it would behoove us to do it well. The best guide I know to readerly judgment is our old friend Auden, who graciously summed up a lifetime of thinking about these matters in a single incisive sentence: "For an adult reader, the possible verdicts are five: I can see this is good and I like it; I can see this is good but I don't like it; I can see this is good, and, though at present I don't like it, I believe with perseverance I shall come to like it; I can see that this is trash but I like it; I can see that this is trash and I don't like it."

Note that Auden separates the act of objective, or at least detached, judgment from the recognition of personal preference.

At least in the immediate term, you can't really decide to like or dislike something: you just know, if you're honest, what response you have. And Auden is encouraging honesty here, especially in acknowledging without disapproval the verdict "I can see that this is trash but I like it." Every one of us pronounces this verdict at some point, though the Vigilant school of critics would like eventually to eliminate it.

But note that Auden does *not* include this option: "I can see that this is trash, and, though at present I like it, I believe with perseverance I shall come to dislike it." This suggests that Auden is un-Vigilant: though he envisions intellectual growth and change, he doesn't associate such growth with acquiring a greater capacity for disapproval. He believes that "perseverance" is a readerly virtue, but wants to direct that perseverance toward a positive union of critical judgment and taste, so that what you see as good in itself you eventually come to enjoy. Auden doesn't want us to scorn "trash" but rather to enjoy more and more of what is good.

However, he also realizes that nobody's taste will ever be all-embracing: therefore he has one category for the recognizably good work that you hope someday to enjoy, but also this: "I can see this is good but I don't like it." Just that, because no matter how hard you try, you won't be able to enjoy everything that is worthy of praise. Nor should you try too hard to achieve such catholicity. In a book review Auden once commented, "No critic will ever amount to much who does not start with strong personal preferences and end by transcending them so that he can see the good in works which are not really his 'dish.' A narrow taste is a bad taste, but a catholic taste which is not arrived at through a process of self-conquest is no taste at all."

For Auden, the robust reader does not begin with complete openness but rather with "strong personal preferences": we do well to be rather narrow in our likes at the outset, but to recognize such narrowness as a trait that *in the long term* becomes a vice. (Remember Voltaire's Venetian count: "'What a superior man!' murmured Candide. 'What a genius this Pococurante is! Nothing can please him.'") Yes, our preferences are limited and always will be: we need not pretend, especially to ourselves, that our scope is greater than it actually is; though pretense to others, as we have noted, is inevitable and sometimes even salutary. No one takes pleasure in every kind of reading, and if we think we do we lack self-knowledge or else have "no taste at all"—no genuine appreciation of anything. But to be satisfied with our own narrowness is just as bad: there is great value in the kind of "self-conquest" that Auden recommends because it is an *expansion of being*, an extension of our lives into realms of experience that we would not know if we did not make the effort to enjoy those works of which our detached critical self approves.

"Everyone's a critic," the saying goes, and it's true: we all make evaluative judgments on what we read. Even as small children we knew what we liked best, what we wanted read to us again and again, and what, conversely, we didn't care to retrieve after a first encounter. Every nursery has its stock of good-as-new books and its (usually smaller) cache of books worn nearly to shreds by sheer love. Our goal as adults is not to love all books alike, or as few as possible, but rather to love as widely and as well as our limited selves will allow.

In solitude, for company ☞ "Our limited selves"—Aye, there's the rub. For many, one of the chief blessings of reading is its power to overcome these limits: David Foster Wallace once said that "the point of books [is] to combat loneliness." Reading is a way of connecting with others, but the connection is an odd combination of the intimate and the virtual: if we say that when Machiavelli entered his study there was *really* no one there, we speak a half-truth. In a way he sat there alone; in another way he enjoyed the best of company.

Many of us form profound attachments when we read. Sometimes we attach ourselves to characters, imagining them as our friends or lovers or most profound enemies; sometimes a book's author draws us, perhaps because of a persona he or she projects, perhaps—especially if we are writers or would-be writers ourselves—because we admire and envy. Nicholson Baker's book *U and I*, concerning his youthful obsession with John Updike, is a funny but also touching account of this kind of connection. Baker would cry out in pleasure after reading one of Updike's famously lapidary sentences; but also, when he read that Updike sometimes golfed with Tim O'Brien, author of *Going After Cacciato*, he thought, "I was of course very hurt that out of all the youngish writers living in the Boston area Updike has chosen Tim O'Brien and not me as his golfing partner. It didn't matter that I hadn't written a book that had won a National Book Award, hadn't written a book of any kind, and didn't know how to golf; still, I felt strongly that Updike should have asked me and not Tim O'Brien."

Which suggests that sometimes, even for the most passionate readers, a rather less virtual connection is wanted. (The young Baker actually stopped reading in the middle of one of Updike's stories and sent the great man a letter of gratitude and admiration.) When I hear from nostalgic former students of mine, what they tend to miss most about their college literature classes is the regular opportunity to talk about books, books that a group of people are all reading at the same time. When I quiz them about this nostalgia, they articulate a rather complex position. They do not say they miss reading highly literary texts; after all, they can do that on their own, and usually do, though a few feel that they lack the discipline to do so as consistently as they want. (At such a juncture I offer my polished-to-a-sheen read-at-whim lecture.) Rather, they miss the conversation that such books generate.

When I ask whether a book group might not be an adequate substitute for the classroom, or even a superior alternative—after all, with no papers to write, grades to receive, and professors to impress, conversations might well be freer and more energetic—they often disagree. Now, it should be said that there may be plenty of other former literature majors who delight in book groups and who, consequently, do not write nostalgic emails to their ex-professors. And more power to them. But those who are not satisfied by book groups tend to give two reasons. The minor one is that the books chosen are rarely challenging enough to provide first-rate conversation. The major one is that too few participants in book groups are interested in really exploring the books: rather, for them, books seem to be an excuse for talking about other matters that they're more deeply interested in, often their own emotional lives.

It seems to me that these two complaints may well be related. Just as a purely entertaining work does not require annotation—does not *bear* annotation—it probably requires little conversation as well. On the other hand, *Finnegans Wake* will not draw a big book-group crowd. The more I think about this, the more I realize how difficult a task book-group leaders, including Oprah Winfrey, have: the book has to be substantive enough to give people something to talk about, but not so difficult that people can't persevere to the end, or that they feel inadequate to the conversation. And if the book is either too simple or too challenging, the most natural thing to do is to fall back on one's *response* to it—on one's own feelings. (Apparent emotivism in this case being a token not of narcissism but of a need to keep a conversation going when the ostensible topic of conversation provides few resources.) In this light it seems wonderful that book groups ever succeed, but succeed they often do—at least for those who want the conversation itself and are willing to allow whatever they read to pass into the background.

But let's imagine a Platonically perfect book group, one that would meet every need of the former literature majors who sometimes write to me with longing for the good old days of college. What would characterize such a group? First and most important, people committed both to careful reading and serious conversation; second, books with sufficient complexity and thoughtfulness to generate significant debate, whether about the works' own structures and procedures or about the issues they raise. Given such circumstances, the solitary act of reading and the communal act of conversing could merge into a single and beautiful entity. Each participant would bring the fruits of his or her private attention to the public table; judgments and interpretations would be tested there, found wanting or found wise, related to the judgments of others. Agreements could be reached, tensions identified—tensions in the group but perhaps also in the texts— and fundamental disagreements could be acknowledged with mutual charity.

The difficulty is to find, in any given place, people who are willing and able to pursue such a noble endeavor, which is why digitally savvy readers are pursuing their connections online. Digital book clubs abound in various forms: sometimes they're named as such; sometimes blogs host "reading events" in which some people are invited to post about a book while everyone is invited to participate in the comments; sometimes the customer-review sections on Amazon.com or other bookselling sites turn into extended debates about the merits of a given text.

One of the most ambitious and promising endeavors in this field is CommentPress, a project of the Institute for the Future of the Book. CommentPress's creators explain that the idea is to take the now-familiar technology of the weblog, "which, most would agree, is very good at covering the present moment in pithy, conversational bursts but lousy at handling larger, slow-developing works requiring more than chronological organization" and adapt it in the hope that "this form might be refashioned to enable social interaction around long-form texts." CommentPress allows readers to comment on a whole book, on a chapter of that book, on a paragraph in that chapter, and, of course, on other comments. It requires a little more thought to participate in a CommentPress conversation than to fire off a reply to a blog post, but that's probably a good thing: the time it takes to think about whether what you want to say is best framed as a comment on a whole book, or on some particular part of it, or as a response to another reader, is time well spent. The idea addressed with precision is more powerful and more meaningful than the idea shot carelessly into (cyber) space. And, of course, thoughtful comments well directed serve writers also.

But virtual communities of this kind may well be experientially closer to reading books than meeting for discussion in a classroom or someone's living room. Participants in online conversations construe one another's characters through the written word in much the same way that Nicholson Baker construed John Updike's character and, on the basis of that construal, wrote him a letter. In the end, it's all *reading*, isn't it? The difference is that the one kind of encounter—Baker's with Updike, for example—is based on one person paying attention to what another is developing over many dozens of pages and thousands of words, while the other is based on back-and-forth exchanges of briefer messages. The online interlocutors can ask and answer questions, which, as Olaudah Equiano learned, doesn't work with books—but then, questions and answers are more necessary in that environment because no one is developing thoughts at great length. If you could get a book to answer your questions, surely it would often say, "Be patient, I'm getting to that."

So whether you're participating in an online conversation or reading a book by yourself, your experience is a readerly one and a responsive one. The most significant difference is that reading a book is dialogically asymmetrical: you learn about the book, about its characters and perhaps its author, but none of them learns anything about you. I'm not convinced that this is *necessarily* regrettable: many of us should probably spend more time just listening, rather than insisting on being heard.

I belabor these points in order to forestall a simplistic conclusion that may be all too tempting in an age of social media. If "social" is intrinsically good, then is not private experience intrinsically less good? This seems to be the view of Steven Johnson, who has expressed great enthusiasm for Amazon.com's "popular highlights" feature, which allows those who highlight passages in the e-books they have bought from Amazon to upload those annotations to Amazon's servers, where they can be compared to the passages other readers have chosen to emphasize. Johnson writes that "with 'popular highlights,' even when we manage to turn off Twitter and the television and sit down to read a good book, there will a chorus of readers turning the pages along with us, pointing out the good bits. Before long, we'll probably be able to meet those fellow readers, share stories with them." And then in relation to a statement I cited at the outset of this section, he adds, "Combating loneliness? David Foster Wallace saw only the half of it." The strong suggestion here is that whatever solitary reading can do to combat loneliness isn't much in comparison to reading with "a chorus of readers turning the pages along with us, pointing out the good bits."

That it's rather hard to read with a chorus echoing in your ears, or high-kicking in the margins of the text like a row of Radio

City Rockettes, doesn't seem to occur to Johnson; nor does the possibility that I might want to make my own decisions about what "the good bits" are. Johnson neglects these points because he is, and has been for many years, an apostle and advocate of "connectedness." Thus, he writes, "Quiet contemplation has led to its fair share of important thoughts. But it cannot be denied that good ideas also emerge in networks."

True: it cannot be denied. But I am not sure who would want to deny it, or who has ever denied it. As far as common sense can tell, every good idea ever achieved is the product of both connection and contemplation, of moving back and forth between the two. Every great thinker has been aware of the work of his or her predecessors and highly responsive to them, and has usually had colleagues as well; and every great thinker has had to retire into solitude, often, in order to think really hard and without interruption. Even a suspicious recluse like Newton valued his interactions with members of the Royal Society, though he also tended to be deeply annoyed by his correspondents' failures to understand him.

Reading too is, or should be, a moving between the solitary encounter and something more social. Even when the "more social" thing is just an entry in a private diary, it constitutes a step away from the silent absorption in a text, an attempt to account for and therefore make one's response more *intersubjective*, that is, connected to, interacting with, the experiences of others. To write a letter to a friend, or participate in an online debate, or join a book group, are all ways of seeking this social dimension of reading, which almost everyone needs to some degree.

But I think I have to insist that these various ways of reading with others are not reading proper, but rather accompaniments to reading. They cannot substitute for the solitary encounter. (Even when we read comments on blog posts, we usually do so silently, and if we're really interested in what the person is saying, we won't want to be interrupted as we read.) These accompaniments change the reading experience in multiple ways: they can force us to reevaluate what we have read, and they can alter our orientation to a text when we go back into our cone of silence. Encounters with other readers can be a vital source of improvements in our judgments, particularly, I think, in teaching us not to be too quickly dismissive: when we hear that others who have been more charitably disposed to a book have gotten something out of it that we missed, we may well be moved to be more charitable ourselves in the future. (I have seen this happen in classroom discussions many times over the years.)

But the question I would put to Stephen Johnson and other celebrants of the connected life is this: in the late modern Western world today, which is in greater danger, the social aspect of our lives or the solitary one? Which suffers from undercultivation? Which is being drowned out by the other? If I have overemphasized the solitary and silent aspects of reading in this book, that may be because I am myself temperamentally inclined to value solitude and silence more than most people, but it is also because they are endangered species of mental experience and because genuine reading is simply impossible without them.

Serendip   ☞ It will be discouraging to some and consoling to others to realize that very little of our growth as readers can be planned. It is certainly possible to read the 189 books Charles Van Doren associates with *The Joy of Reading*, the 173 indispensables that he and Mortimer Adler list at the end of *How to Read a Book*, and most certainly the sixteen texts that Michael Dirda says will open the world of literature to you—but it is not possible to acquire by force of will the enjoyment of all of them, or any.

The "self-conquest" Auden recommends will always be achieved, when it is achieved at all, by hook or by crook, unmethodically, unpredictably. We must consent to be guided by the invisible hand of serendipity.

The word was coined by that curious man Sir Horace Walpole, known today (if at all) as one of the founders of the "Gothic" tale of suspense and terror, but more famous in his own time as an especially elegant and proficient writer of letters. In a 1754 letter to a friend he describes his discovery of some curious Venetian coat of arms and pauses to say that "this discovery, indeed, is almost of that kind which I call Serendipity." And then he explains this "very expressive word" of his own invention: "I once read a silly fairy tale, called 'The Three Princes of Serendip' "—Serendip being an old name for Sri Lanka: "as their Highnesses travelled, they were always making discoveries, by accidents and sagacity, of things which they were not in quest of . . . (for you must observe that no discovery of a thing you are looking for comes under this description)." The finding of what one is not looking for will be the element of the letter most obviously relevant to what I've been saying so far; but equally important is the phrase "by accidents and sagacity," or, as Walpole puts it later in the same letter, "accidental sagacity."

Fortuity happens, but serendipity can be cultivated. You can grow in serendipity. You can even become a disciple of serendipity. In the literature of the Middle Ages, we see reverence for the goddess Fortuna—fortune, chance—and to worship her is a religious way of shrugging: an admission of helplessness, an acknowledgment of all that lies beyond our powers of control. But in the very idea of serendipity is a kind of hope, even an expectation, that we can turn the accidents of fortune to good account, and make of them some knowledge that would have been inaccessible to us if we had done no more than find what we were looking for. Indeed, it may be possible not only to cultivate the sagacity but also the accidents. It may be possible, and desirable, to actively put yourself in the way of events beyond your control.

It is often said that the Internet—especially Google search— marks the end of serendipity. I used to think this myself. For instance, I once wrote, in an essay about dictionaries, "Surely every user of dictionaries or encyclopedias can recall many serendipitous discoveries: as we flip through pages in search of some particular chunk of information, our eyes are snagged by some oddity, some word or phrase or person or place, unlooked-for but all the more irresistible for that. On my way to 'serendipity' I trip over 'solleret,' and discover that those weird, broad metal shoes that I've seen on the feet of armored knights have a name. But this sort of thing never happens to me when I look up a word in an online dictionary. The blessing of Google is its uncanny skill in finding what you're looking for; the curse is that it so rarely finds any of those lovely odd things you're *not* looking for." But I don't say this kind of thing any more, because I have realized just how much serendipity has come my way through just *clicking on links*. (I found many of the most incisive quotations in this book that way.)

And specifically in relation to reading, I am endlessly fascinated by a feature on Amazon.com: "People Who Bought This Item Also Bought. . . ." Most of the time this information is as obvious as can be: People who bought Tolkien's *The Fellowship of the Ring* also bought *The Two Towers*! But if you keep clicking through those lists you can come across some surprising and even inexplicable results. For instance, I learned today that purchasers of my book *Original Sin: A Cultural History* also bought Cicero's treatise *On the Good Life*. Surely that was just one person—Amazon doesn't make that clear—but what a curious pairing. . . . And it occurs to me that I don't know what Cicero thinks the good life is all about, and that it might be interesting to find out.

I find such suggestions irresistible, even when they are auto-suggestions, which is why, I think, I have come so passionately to distrust reading lists. I used to try to determine in advance what books I would read over the summer, but eventually realized that to put *any* book on such a list nearly guaranteed that I would not read it. No matter how anxiously I had been anticipating it, as soon as it took its place among the other assigned texts it became as broccoli unto me—and any book *not* on the list, no matter how unattractive it might appear in other contexts, immediately became as desirable as a hot fudge sundae. And over the years I have decided that this instinctive resistance to the predetermined is a gift, not a disability.

The cultivation of serendipity is an option for anyone, but for people living in conditions of prosperity and security and informational richness it is something vital. To practice "accidental sagacity" is to recognize that I don't really know where I am going, even if I like to think I do, or think Google does; that if I know what I am looking for, I do not therefore know what I need; that I am not master of my destiny and captain of my fate; that it is probably a very good thing that I am not master of my destiny and captain of my fate. An *accidental* sagacity may be the form of wisdom I most need, but am least likely to find without eager pursuit. Moreover, serendipity is the near relation of Whim; each stands against the Plan.

Plan once appealed to me, but I have grown to be a natural worshiper of Serendipity and Whim; I can *try* to serve other gods, but my heart is never in it. I truly think I would rather read an indifferent book on a lark than a fine one according to schedule and plan. And why not? After all, once upon a time we chose none of our reading: it all came to us unbidden, unanticipated, unknown, and from the hand of someone who loved us.

How it all started ☞ As this narrative moves toward its close, let's return to those early experiences of being read to, of sitting next to someone who loves us and fixing our eyes on the page. In *Proust and the Squid*, Maryann Wolf notes that for many children the act of being read to—and therefore the book itself—is powerfully associated with being *loved*. And that association does not cease at this stage: as the novelist Penelope Fitzgerald has commented, "Twice in your life you know you are approved of by everyone—when you learn to walk and when you learn to read."

Learning to read is indeed a momentous achievement, and many adults can remember a good deal about climbing that mountain. Fitzgerald again: "I began to read just after I was four. The letters on the page suddenly gave in and admitted what they stood for. They obliged me completely and all at once." A miracle! Graham Greene's memory told him the same story of instantaneous mastery: "I remember distinctly the suddenness with which a key turned in a lock and I found I could read—not just the sentences in a reading book with the syllables coupled like railway carriages, but a real book. It was paper-covered with the picture of a boy, bound and gagged, dangling at the end of a rope inside a well with the water rising above his waist—an adventure of Dixon Brett, detective."

But Greene's sudden empowerment was accompanied by something far less pleasant: fear, foreboding.

> All a long summer holiday I kept my secret, as I believed: I did not want anybody to know that I could read. I suppose I half consciously realized even then that this was the dangerous moment. I was safe so long as I could not read—the wheels had not begun to turn, but now the future stood around on bookshelves everywhere waiting for the child to choose—the life of a chartered accountant

perhaps, a colonial civil servant, a planter in China, a steady job in a bank. . . . I suppose my mother must have discovered my secret, for on the journey home I was presented for the train with another real book, a copy of [R. M.] Ballantyne's *Coral Island* with only a single picture to look at, a coloured frontispiece. But I would admit nothing. All the long journey I stared at the one picture and never opened the book.

Similarly, the son of one of my friends was slow to learn to read, despite obvious intelligence; this puzzled and troubled his parents for some time, until finally the poor boy confessed that he was afraid that if he learned to read his father would no longer read books *to* him at bedtime. Only after repeated and vigorous reassurances would he consent to allow the new, fearful knowledge to enter in.

School brings more reading-related tensions, since one's place in a class can be determined by one's reading ability: "Which reading group are you in?" But school is also the place where comfort with reading tends to be confirmed. In school, then, reading gets linked to a zig-zagging alternation between empowerment and anxiety, an alternation that for some people can last a lifetime. Erin O'Connor, who has taught English literature at the University of Pennsylvania and also at the high school level, precisely notes the difficulties here, echoing a number of points we have emphasized in these pages:

English teachers are mediators. They are not ends in themselves. That's how it should be, anyway. They are training wheels that young readers ought to be able to shed once they acquire the skills they need to read purposefully and profitably on their own. But, too often, this backfires. Kids get turned off, and reading just becomes a chore they have to do for school. Or—and this pattern is less discussed, but still troubling—they become dependent. They may really enjoy reading—but they think they need a class, and spoonfed lectures, and guided discussions, in order to get anything out of what they read. They are willing and eager—but have learned from their teachers exactly what they should not have learned. They have become passive where they should be active, and the teacher becomes a crutch for laziness, fear, uncertainty, and sometimes even a creeping snobbery about reading, about choosing what to read, deciding how to read, and figuring out what one thinks about what one has read. These folks grow up into the kind of adults who answer questions about their favorite books by listing works they think *should* be their favorites—but that they may never have even actually read.

So reading, which starts for many of us in a warm cocoon of security, accompanied by an unassailable sense of being loved, gradually and inexorably—Gibbon would say *insensibly*—turns into a site of stress. It becomes a contested environment in which we succeed or fail, perhaps all alone; and that unwanted solitude causes us to reattach ourselves, or keep ourselves attached, to others who can both direct and validate. And to lie, to others and perhaps ourselves, about who we really are as readers and therefore as persons.

In these circumstances, that anyone ever becomes a *reader*—someone who does it because she loves it and can't help herself—is something close to a miracle. Yet this happens and happens powerfully (thus, the title of Francis Spufford's memoir: *The Child That Books Built: A Life in Reading*.) And it may be that when we first emerge from that comforting cocoon of being-read-to we are especially sensitive to what books and stories offer. Thus, Greene's speculation: "Perhaps it is only in childhood that books have any deep influence on our lives.

In later life we admire, we are entertained, we may modify some views we already hold, but we are more likely to find in books merely a confirmation of what is in our minds already." This is needlessly morose, as is characteristic of Greene: we may be tempted to use books and other texts as ways of confirming our self-images, but the temptation *can* be resisted. Nevertheless, it's surely true that in childhood, when we first take the book into our own hands and sit by ourselves with it, we (as Elizabeth Bowen put it) truly and fully "come across." That so many of us conquer our fears of being cut off and embrace this solitude—this solitude that is also a connection—suggests that the rewards of reading can be considerable indeed.

Throughout this book, I have repeatedly tried to identify those rewards, to separate them from all those comforts and anxieties, those self-condemnations and self-congratulations, that accompany the experience. I have also tried to acknowledge the dangers and impediments to the concentration serious reading needs, without exaggerating them. It is possible to ignore such dangers—say, by convincing yourself that you are a massively skilled multitasker— but it is equally easy to magnify their power until resistance seems futile. We should rather remember that it is possible and, really, necessary to do what David Foster Wallace recommended to the graduates of Kenyon: to be "conscious and aware enough to *choose* what you pay attention to and to choose how you construct meaning from experience."

To pick up a book—to decide to read something, almost anything—is to choose a particular form of attention. That choice creates simultaneously silence and receptiveness to a voice; the reader acts imaginatively, constructing meaning from the experience of finding words on a page, but also, ideally, strives to assume a posture of charity toward what he or she reads. This choosing reader is never merely passive, never simply a consumer, but constantly engages in critical judgment, sometimes with-holding sympathy with a thoughtful wariness, and then, in the most blessed moments, when trust has been earned, giving that sympathy wholly and without stint.

About seven hundred years ago Richard de Bury—an English monk, librarian, book collector, and eventually Bishop of Durham—wrote that "in books I find the dead as if they were alive; in books I foresee things to come; in books warlike affairs are set forth; from books come forth the laws of peace. All things are corrupted and decay in time; Saturn ceases not to devour the children that he generates; all the glory of the world would be buried in oblivion, unless God had provided mortals with the remedy of books." An effusive encomium to the joys and benefits of reading, yes, but not *too* effusive. Richard's bookish, readerly community, extending through time and across space, has still a substantial membership; nonread-ers outnumber us—always have and always will—but we can always find one another and are always eager to welcome others into the fold. May our tribe increase.

AN ESSAY ON SOURCES

Yes, We Can! ☞ The revised edition of *How to Read a Book*, coauthored by Van Doren, came out in 1972; that version is still in print today (New York: Touchstone Books) and sells healthily. Steve Jobs announced that no one reads anymore in an interview published in the January 15, 2008, edition of the *New York Times*. The phrase "Dumbest Generation" comes from a book by Mark Bauerlein, the full title of which is *The Dumbest Generation: How the Digital Age Stupefies Young Americans and Jeopardizes Our Future* (New York: Penguin, 2008). Unsurprisingly, the book's cover features a warmly morose commendation from Harold Bloom: "An urgent and pragmatic book on the very dark topic of the virtual end of reading among the young."

Nicholas Carr's lament for his old brain may be found in his book *The Shallows: What the Internet Is Doing to Our Brains* (New York: W. W. Norton, 2010). I will refer to this thoughtful but perhaps overly pessimistic book several times in the pages that follow. It was Carr who called my attention to "Reading and the Reading Class in the Twenty-First Century," the article by Wendy Griswold, Terry McDonnell, and Nathan Wright, three sociologists from Northwestern University, that among other things reports on the remarkably positive American attitudes toward reading (*Annual Review of Sociology* 31: 127–41).

I mention Mark Dirda's *Book by Book: Notes on Reading and Life* (New York: Henry Holt, 2005) only to criticize one small passage from it, but it's a delightful account in many ways and very much worth reading. Similarly, while the how-to approach taken by Thomas Foster in his *How to Read Literature Like a Professor* (New York: Harper, 2003) and *How to Read Novels Like a Professor* (2008) just sets my teeth on edge, I know that that's *my* problem: these are genial and for many readers quite helpful books. Zadie Smith's comment on a very different kind of professor comes from an interview with her I discovered on Penguin's Web site dedicated to her book *On Beauty*: http://us.penguingroup.com/static/rguides/us/on_beauty.html.

Whim ☞ The essay by Kipling that I cite in this section and elsewhere is called "The Uses of Reading": it was originally a talk given at Wellington College and was later printed in a collection called *A Book of Words* (1928). Richard Rodriguez's *Hunger of Memory: The Autobiography of Richard Rodriguez* (New York: Bantam, 1982) is now rightly seen as a classic of American memoir. Randall Jarrell's great commendation of whim—so influential in the pages that follow—appears in an essay called "Poets, Critics, and Readers," reprinted in *No Other Book: Selected Essays*, edited by Brad Leithauser (New York: Harper, 1999).

C. S. Lewis's savagely witty comment on reading as "social and ethical hygiene" may be found in his *An Experiment in Criticism* (Cambridge: Cambridge University Press, 1961). Ray Suarez interviewed Harold Bloom about Harry Potter in 2000: http://www.pbs.org/newshour/conversation/july-dec00/bloom_8-29.html. His comments on the only American writers that "deserve our praise" appeared in the *Boston Globe* on September 24, 2003: http://www.boston.com/news/globe/editorial_opinion/oped/articles/2003/09/24/dumbing_down_american_readers/. His *How to Read and Why* was published in 2001 (New York: Scribner). Professor Williamson's despair over students who aren't sufficiently ashamed of their trashy reading appeared in a story by Ron Charles in the *Washington Post* (Sunday, March 8, 2009), "On Campus, Vampires Are Besting the Beats." I learned about Dwight Macdonald's repudiation of the motivating power of shame in "Bring Back Dwight!" an essay by John Summers that was posted on the Web site of the *New Republic* on January 20, 2010: http://www.tnr.com/book/review/bring-back-dwight.

The interview with LCD Soundsystem's James Murphy that I quote appeared in the *Guardian* of London on April 24, 2010: http://www.guardian. co.uk/music/2010/apr/24/lcd-soundsystem-this-is-happening. Chesterton's wonderful essay "In Defence of Penny Dreadfuls" (1901) may be found in dozens of places on the Internet. Auden's comment on the "high holidays of the spirit" comes from his essay called simply "Reading," in *The Dyer's Hand* (New York: Random House, 1962). Walter Kirn's *Lost in the Meritocracy: The Undereducation of an Overachiever* (New York: Doubleday) came out in 2009. Cathleen Schine's essay "I Was a Teenage Illiterate" appeared in the *New York Times Book Review* on February 26, 2010: http://www.nytimes.com/2010/02/28/ books/review/Schine-t.html.

All in your head ☞ Pinker's statement about the "bolting on" of writing appears in his "Foreword" to Diane McGuinness's *Why Our Children Can't Read: And What We Can Do About It* (New York: Free Press, 1997). A. D. Nuttall's provocative *Why Does Tragedy Give Pleasure?* (New York: Oxford University Press) appeared in 1996. "If we were all wicked, there would perhaps be no problem. A world of torturers would naturally be pleased by the blinding of Oedipus.... But why does tragedy give pleasure to 'people like ourselves'?" Maryanne Wolf's *Proust and the Squid* (New York: Harper, 2008) and Stanislas Dehaene's *Reading in the Brain* (New York: Viking, 2009) are both wonderful books that give generally similar accounts of the state of research into how brains read—but there *are* differences, and when they occur I have no way of knowing whose account to prefer.

Dr. Johnson's account of his pain on reading of Cordelia's death may be found in his notes to *King Lear* in his great edition of Shakespeare's plays (1765).

Aspirations ☞ Neil Gaiman confessed his devotion to the Narnia books in his Guest of Honor speech at Mythcon 35 (the annual meet- ing of the Mythopoeic Society) in 2004: http://www.mythsoc.org/ mythcon/35/speech/. Michael Chabon's celebration of the "bliss" of influence appears in his essay "Fan Fiction: On Sherlock Holmes," reprinted in his delightful collection *Maps and Legends* (San Francisco: McSweeney's Books, 2008). I don't remember where I first came across the Churchill– Stafford Cripps anecdote. Alex Rose's "at least they're watching TV" line appeared on the blog of the Institute for the Future of the Book: http://www.futureofthebook.org/blog/archives/2009/07/the_almighty_word.html.

Gibbon wrote his *Autobiography* in the last years of his life; it was published in 1795, the year after his death. William Gaddis's *The Recognitions* appeared in 1955; some recent editions come in at less than a thousand pages, which almost makes me think I could try it again.

Upstream   ☞ Lowes's *The Road to Xanadu* appears to be in print, though in an expensive edition published by an outfit called Dyer Press. There are several versions of *Bartram's Travels* available, including a Library of America edition (1996). My favorite translation of *Sir Gawain and the Green Knight* is that of Simon Armitage (New York: W. W. Norton, 2007); think of it as the ideal bookend to Seamus Heaney's great version of *Beowulf* (2001), from the same publisher. The quotation from Hume is taken from his *Enquiry Concerning Human Understanding* (1748), his attempt to make some of his earlier philosophical work more accessible.

Responsiveness   ☞ Machiavelli's account of his decorous library behavior comes from a letter to Francesco Vettori, as printed in *The Literary Works of Machiavelli*, edited by J. R. Hale (Oxford: Oxford University Press, 1961). Terry Eagleton's puncturing of the idea that high culture automatically produces moral excellence may be found in his *Literary Theory: an Introduction*, Anniversary Edition (Minneapolis: University of Minnesota Press, 2008). Auden loved to quote Lichtenberg's line about mirrors and asses; I got it from him. Brendan Gill's anecdote about John O'Hara is one of the many juicy ones from his memoir *Here at the New Yorker* (New York: Random House, 1975). Mikhail Bakhtin articulates his idea about the primacy of response in communication in his long essay from the 1930s, "Discourse in the Novel," which is found in *The Dialogic Imagination*, translated by Caryl Emerson and Michael Holquist (Austin: University of Texas Press, 1981). Alberto Manguel's comment on the generosity of readers is taken from his celebrated *History of Reading* (New York: Viking Press, 1996).

The Interesting Narrative of the Life of Olaudah Equiano, or Gustavus Vassa, the African was published in 1789 and became quite popular, going through several editions. Charles Simic's account of his strong opinions on annotation appeared on the blog of the *New York Review of Books* on December 14,

2009: http://blogs.nybooks.com/post/283414678/on-the-couch-with-philip-roth-at-the-morgue-with-pol. I learned about Jeremias Drexel's similarly strict commitment to annotation from the historian Ann Blair, whom I will cite again later in this book. As I write, her book *Too Much to Know: Managing Scholarly Information before the Modern Age* has not yet appeared, but I eagerly await its appearance. Here I have relied primarily on her article "Reading Strategies for Coping with Information Overload, ca. 1550–1700," *Journal of the History of Ideas* 64:1 (January 2003). Keith Thomas's characteristically delightful meditation on note-taking and the varieties of scholarly organization appeared as a "Diary" entry in the *London Review of Books* 32:11 (10 June 2010).

Slowly, slowly ☞ If you simply must find out more about *bkkeepr*, the URL is http://bkkeepr.com/. I would prefer not to offer any more information than I already have about Peter Boxall's *1001 Books You Must Read Before You Die*, and if you don't also know about *1001 Paintings You Must See Before You Die*, *1001 Movies You Must See Before You Die*, and so on, you didn't hear about them from me. On an equally depressing note, most of the work of the extraordinary R. A. Lafferty is out of print; I don't think it would be easy to find "The Primary Education of the Camiroi," which was first published in 1966 and then reprinted in Lafferty's collection of short fiction *Nine Hundred Grandmothers* (the title story of which is another little masterpiece).

I cannot now recall whether I came across Don Tapscott's *Grown Up Digital: How the Net Generation Is Changing Your World* (New York: McGraw-Hill, 2009) on my own or whether I read about it in something by Nicholas Carr. Probably the latter, but it's certain that when I had forgotten where I read about Joe O'Shea one of my blog readers, Scott Howard, tracked down the quote for me. Geoff Nicholson's story about his reading competition with his friend Rob appeared in the *New York Times Book Review* on February 19, 2009: http://www.nytimes.com/2009/02/22/books/review/Nicholson-t.html. The full title of Martin Amis' novel is *Money: A Suicide Note* (New York: Viking, 1985; first published in the United Kingdom in 1984).

True confessions ☞ William James gave us that memorable phrase about our infant consciousness in his *Principles of Psychology* (1890).

Christine Rosen's essay "People of the Screen" appeared in the Fall 2008 issue of *The New Atlantis*. Sam Anderson's "In Defense of Distraction"—almost the opposite of Rosen's essay—appeared in the May 25, 2009 issue of *New York*; Cory Doctorow's line about "interruption technologies" may be found here: http://www.locusmag.com/Features/2009/01/cory-doctorow-writing-in-age-of.html. A good general account of the recent research on multitasking's problematic cognitive consequences may be found in an article entitled "Hooked on Gadgets, and Paying a Mental Price," in the June 6, 2010, edition of the *New York Times*. In his book *The Myth of Multitasking: How "Doing It All" Gets Nothing Done* (San Francisco: Jossey-Bass, 2008), Dave Crenshaw points out that genuine multitasking is actually impossible and suggests the more accurate alternative term "switchtasking."

A lightly edited version of the commencement address David Foster Wallace gave at Kenyon College in 2005 appeared in the *Wall Street Journal* on September 19, 2008, just a few days after Wallace's heart-rending death by his own hand.

Lost   ☞ Winifred Gallagher's *Rapt: Attention and the Focused Life* (New York: Penguin, 2009) would have been a very good book had it not been cast in a hortatory life-coach mode. That tone grates. I actually learned more about these matters from Maggie Jackson's *Distracted: The Erosion of Attention and the Coming Dark Age* (New York: Prometheus Books, 2008), though I did not end up quoting it in these pages.

Auden's "*Horae Canonicae*"—seven linked poems, each named after one of the monastic hours—appear in both his *Collected Poems* (New York: Modern Library, 2007) and *Selected Poems* (New York: Vintage, 2007). He worked on these poems between 1949 and 1954, and they constitute, I think, his finest achievement as a poet. My quotations are from the third of the poems, "Sext"; one of my later sections takes its title from the refrain of the last poem, "Lauds": "In solitude, for company."

I found the anecdote about Cobbett's discovery of Swift in Margaret Willes's fine book *Reading Matters: Five Centuries of Discovering Books* (New Haven: Yale University Press, 2008). Lynne Sharon Schwartz's *Ruined by Reading: A Life in Books* (Boston: Beacon Press, 1996) is a wise and funny account of one reader's life. In the latter part of this book I quote several times from Jonathan Rose's *The Intellectual Life of the British Working Classes* (New Haven: Yale University Press, 2001) and would have done so a dozen more times if due proportion had allowed. A second edition has just appeared (2010).

Abbot Hugh's advice ☞ Almost everything I know about Hugh of St. Victor I learned, as I note in the text, from Ivan Illich's astonishing book *In the Vineyard of the Text: A Commentary to Hugh's Didascalicon* (Chicago: University of Chicago Press, 1996). I cannot recommend it too highly. Illich led me to Jerome Taylor's translation of the *Didascalicon* (New York: Columbia University Press, 1961, 1991). There's a fine translation of Josek Pieper's *On Hope* by Sister Mary Frances McCarthy (San Francisco: Ignatius Press, 1986).

Charles Simic's celebration of the state of poetry in America comes in another of his entries on the *New York Review of Books* blog: http://www.nybooks.com/blogs/nyrblog/2010/apr/27/confessions-of-a-poet-laureate/. W. S. Merwin's "Why Some People Do Not Read Poetry" also appeared in the *New York Review of Books*, the print edition of April 30, 2009.

The triumphant return of Adler and Van Doren ☞ What we now call Darwin's *Autobiography* Darwin himself called "Recollections of the Development of my Mind and Character," intending it only for his family to read. His son Francis published an edited version in 1902.

Plastic attention ☞ Here again I am drawing on Nicholas Carr's *The Shallows*, mentioned above. The book by Norman Doidge he cites is *The Brain That Changes Itself: Stories of Personal Triumph from the Frontiers of Brain Science* (New York: Viking, 2008). Clay Shirky's dismissal of *War and Peace* came during an exchange with Carr on the Encyclopedia Britannica blog in July of 2008: http://www.britannica.com/blogs/2008/07/why-abundance-is-good-a-reply-to-nick-carr/. Each entry in the exchange is worth reading.

N. Katherine Hayles's article "Hyper and Deep Attention: The Generational Divide in Cognitive Modes" appeared in the Modern Language Association's annual *Profession* (2007). She was quoted on contemporary pedagogical challenges in an article called "Divided Attention," by David Glenn, in the *Chronicle Review* (January 31, 2010).

Getting schooled ☞ I cite the article by Wendy Griswold, Terry McDonnell, and Nathan Wright in the notes to the first section, above. Peter Brown's *Augustine of Hippo: A Biography*, revised edition

(Berkeley: University of California Press, 2000) is the best available and a model of biographical tact and scholarly depth. George Steiner celebrates Erasmus in an essay called "The End of Bookishness?" (*Times Literary Supplement*, July 8–14, 1988). All my comments about early modern scholarly practice here are derived from the article by Ann Blair mentioned above.

Clay Shirky's great line about "filter failure" comes from a talk he gave at the Web 2.0 Expo in New York on September 19, 2008. Shreeharsh Kelkar commented on his blog: http://cogsciresearch.blogspot.com/2008/08/in-praise-of-skimming-response-to.html. Peter Norvig was quoted on the coexistence of concentrating and skimming in an article by Nate Anderson on the Ars Technica website with the unfortunate title "Sorry, English Major, the Engineers Have Triumphed": http://arstechnica.com/tech-policy/news/2010/02/sorry-english-major-the-engineers-have-triumphed.ars. I refuse to admit defeat, even though I don't know what war I'm fighting and how the engineers ended up on the other side.

John Milton's "Of Education" was printed in 1644.

Quiet, please ☞ George Prochnik's explanation for why he wrote *In Pursuit of Silence: Listening for Meaning in a World of Noise* (New York: Doubleday, 2010) appeared on the Amazon.com page for the book. Bernard Knox's "Silent Reading in Antiquity" appeared in *Greek, Roman, and Byzantine Studies* 9 (1968). Paul Saenger develops his argument about the emergence of silent reading in monastic culture in his *Space between Words: The Origins of Silent Reading* (Stanford, Calif.: Stanford University Press, 2000). Bruce R. Smith's *The Acoustic World of Early Modern England* (Chicago: University of Chicago Press, 1999) is quite dense but unusually thought-provoking; the same can be said for Diana Webb's *Privacy and Solitude in the Middle Ages* (London: Hambledon and London, 2007).

Victoria Coren's dissent from Andy Burnham's library plan appeared in London's Sunday *Observer* (October 12, 2008); Charlotte Leslie's in the *Guardian* (October 13, 2008). Paul Bloom's article "The Pleasures of Imagination" appeared in the May 30, 2010, issue of the *Chronicle Review*; it is adapted from his book *How Pleasure Works: The New Science of Why We Like What We Like* (New York: W. W. Norton, 2010).

The lovely essay "Out of a Book" may be found in *The Mulberry Tree: Writings of Elizabeth Bowen*, edited by Hermione Lee (New York: Harcourt, 1987).

One of my favorite memoirs—though it may be more essay than memoir—is Francis Spufford's *The Child That Books Built: A Life In Reading* (London: Faber and Faber, 2002). I am pleased to have the chance to quote it here, and had to resist, strongly, the temptation to do so a dozen more times.

Once more, with feeling   ☞ Chesterton's *The Man Who Was Thursday* appeared in 1907; many editions are available, including free ones online. Auden's "A Knight of Doleful Countenance" appeared in the *New Yorker* (May 25, 1968) and was later reprinted in his *Forewords and Afterwords* (New York: Random House, 1972) with the subtitle "Second Thoughts on Kierkegaard." L. E. Sissman's image of the clearing in the forest comes from one of his "Innocent Bystander" columns from *The Atlantic*, collected in the volume *Innocent Bystander: The Scene from the 70's* (New York: Vanguard Press, 1975). I discovered this quotation at Patrick Kurp's blog Anecdotal Evidence: http://evidenceanecdotal.blogspot.com/2008/08/clearing-in-forest .html.

Walter Benjamin's "The Storyteller: Reflections on the Works of Nikolai Leskov" appears in his posthumous collection *Illuminations*, translated by Harry Zohn (New York: Schocken Books, 1968). Auden's five possible readerly verdicts are listed in his *A Certain World: A Commonplace Book* (London: Faber and Faber, 1970); his insistence on critical "self-conquest" comes from a review, published in *The Griffin* (March 1956), of C. S. Lewis's *English Literature in the Sixteenth Century, Excluding Drama*.

In solitude, for company   ☞ According to David Lipsky in *Although of Course You End Up Becoming Yourself: A Road Trip with David Foster Wallace* (New York: Broadway Books, 2010), Wallace proposed the idea that "the point of books was to combat loneliness" in a conversation with Jonathan Franzen in 1995, when both of them were early in their writing careers. Nicholson Baker's *U and I* (New York: Random House, 1991) is quite funny and uncomfortably insightful about the ways that writers relate to other writers, especially ones they admire.

The CommentPress mission statement—written, I assume, by Kathleen Fitzpatrick, the leading figure in the project—may be found here: http:// mediacommons.futureofthebook.org/mcpress/cpfinal/introduction/. More people should know about this project. The essay by Steven Johnson that

I cite is called "Yes, People Still Read, but Now It's Social," and, interestingly, it appeared in the Business section of the *New York Times* (June 18, 2010).

Serendip ☞ Sir Horace Walpole (1717–1797), though he wrote one of the earlier "Gothic" novels, *The Castle of Otranto*, was most successful as a designer of his own home (the legendary Strawberry Hill in Twickenham, west of London) and as the writer of thousands of wonderfully well-crafted letters. Some reputable publisher really needs to offer a selection of them, but you can find the whole collection at Project Gutenberg. He coined the term "serendipity" in a letter to his friend Horace Mann (January 28, 1754).

How it all started ☞ Penelope Fitzgerald's tender recollection of being "approved of by everyone" may be found in her essay "Why I Write," which is included in the collection of her occasional prose *A House of Air* (New York: Harper Perennial, 2009 [2003]). I found the quotation I use in Maryanne Wolf's *Proust and the Squid*. Graham Greene's account of his origins as a reader may be found in *The Lost Childhood and Other Essays* (New York: Viking, 1952). Erin O'Connor's grief for what happens when the teaching of literature goes astray appears on her blog: http://www.erinoconnor.org/archives/2009/01/poe_prompt.html.

I cannot now recall how I was led to my concluding quotation, but some time back I discovered *The Love of Books: Being the Philobiblon of Richard de Bury*, translated by E. C. Thomas (London: De La More Press, 1903) on Google Books. For this kind of otherwise obscure text, Google Books is a great treasure-house. Richard de Bury was born in 1281 and died in 1345.

ACKNOWLEDGMENTS

☞ Whom to thank in a book about reading? My parents, for teaching me to read? People who over the years have recommended books to me that ended up changing my life? Yes and yes, but if I'm not careful there'll be no end to it. My dedication indicates one key debt that I am particularly pleased to acknowledge; and now, governed by a commitment to radical selectivity, I move on to a few others:

Cynthia Read, my editor, who encouraged this project, supported it, made corrections, asked for clarifications, suggested anecdotes, and corresponded cheerfully and helpfully through the whole process of writing;

Everyone else associated with Oxford University Press, whose professionalism and courtesy have been exemplary;

Christy Fletcher, my agent, who has made this writer's life easier in *so* many ways;

Susan Holman, Tim Larsen, Bryan McGraw, Dan Treier, and John Wilson, who read a late draft of the book and offered tremendously helpful advice (which I usually, but not always, took);

Readers of and commenters upon my blog Text Patterns (http://text-patterns.thenewatlantis.com/), where many of the ideas in this book were first tried out;

My wife Teri and son Wesley, who, throughout the writing of this book, offered support, relief, encouragement, good cheer, and all the other blessed forms of familial love;

And finally, the participants in the Virginia seminar of the Project on Lived Theology: the aforementioned Susan Holman, Carlos Eire, Mark Gornik, Patricia Hampl, Charles Marsh (impresario and convener), and Chuck Mathewes. Perhaps only they will understand the sense in which this book is an exercise in lived theology. Their fellowship over the past few years has been deeply meaningful to me, and I hope and trust that our bonds will continue to be strong in the years to come.